Dauphiné

*This book is dedicated to Ella Laszlo and
Enid and Archie Morison, and to the
memory of Elizabeth Fodor (1890–1990).*

PATHMASTER GUIDES

CIRCULAR 30 WALKS FROM REGIONAL CENTRES

DAUPHINÉ

Ilona Bellos & Hugh Morison

Series Editor
Richard Sale

The Crowood Press

First published in 1991 by
The Crowood Press Ltd
Gipsy Lane
Swindon
SN2 6DQ

©The Crowood Press Ltd 1991

British Library Cataloguing in Publication Data
Bellos, Ilona
    Dauphiné : 30 circular walks from regional centres. -
    (Pathmaster guide series).
    1. France. Dauphiné - Visitor's guides
    I. Title   II. Morison, Hugh   III. Series
    914.49604839

    ISBN 1 85223 441 5

Picture Credits
Black and white photographs throughout, and cover photographs by the authors; drawings by Gareth Davies; all maps by Malcolm Walker.

Acknowledgements
The authors would like to thank Marie-Paule Castaignet for advice on walks, John King for help with photography and Ella Laszlo for hospitality.

In places times from timetables and certain costs, including fares, have been quoted. These were correct at time of going to press, but it cannot be guaranteed that they will remain the same in subsequent years.

Typeset by Carreg Limited, Nailsea, Bristol
Printed in Great Britain by Redwood Press Ltd, Melksham, Wilts

CONTENTS

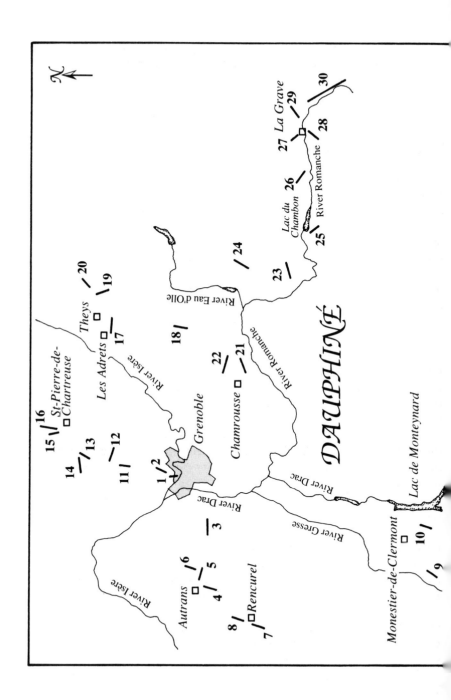

DAUPHINÉ

N

St-Pierre-de-Chartreuse
Theys
Les Adrets
Grenoble
Chamrousse
Autrans
Rencurel
Monestier-de-Clermont
La Grave
Lac du Chambon
Lac de Monteynard

River Isère
River Drac
River Gresse
River Drac
River Romanche
River Eau d'Olle
River Romanche
River Isère

15 16
14 13
11 12
1 2
3
6
5
4
8 7
17
18
20 19
22 21
24
23
26
27 29 30
28
25
10
9

INTRODUCTION

The Dauphiné for Walkers

When asked whether he ever took any vigorous outdoor exercise, Oscar Wilde replied, 'Yes, I occasionally play dominoes sitting outside a French café'. The Dauphiné offers the walker the chance to do just that on terraces with some of the most spectacular views in Europe, together with a variety of walks ranging from the simple to the strenuous, and suitable for everyone from the inexperienced to the most expert Munro bagger.

The Dauphiné contains four mountain ranges: the Vercors and Trièves (to the south-west of Grenoble); the heavily wooded Chartreuse (to the north); the Massif de Belledonne (to the east); and the Massif de l'Oisans, which includes the highest peaks (to the south-east). All contain a great variety of walks in terms of both scenery and difficulty, and any one of them would be suitable as a centre for a week or two's walking. The walks in this book have been organised round the four ranges with a section on each, following the description of two popular walks in the environs of Grenoble to give you an opportunity to orient yourself and to form an impression of the region as a whole.

So, what is the attraction of the Dauphiné? First, there is the scenery – steep valleys, thickly wooded slopes, little hamlets perched beside mountain streams and of course the high peaks, the eternal snows and – in l'Oisans – the glaciers. It is not necessary to don ropes and pitons to reach the high meadows (none of the walks in this book require specialist equipment or skills), yet the rewards are spectacular.

Secondly, the whole region is crisscrossed by a network of paths, many of them waymarked. The region is traversed by a number of national Grandes Randonnées (GR), national long-distance footpaths, including GR54, which offers a five-day circuit of l'Oisans. (Booklets about the GR can be obtained from the Maison de la Randonnée, see 'Preparations…' on p.21.) In addition there are many local paths, kept in good order by the community and, in some places, by Alpine troops. In many areas there are excellently produced topo-guides, available at the local Syndicat d'Initiative or tourist office, which give suggestions for walks in the locality.

Thirdly, there is the wildlife. While there are fewer birds than you might have expected (the French habit of taking a pot shot at anything with feathers has taken its toll), you will certainly meet Alpine choughs and the occasional buzzard and peregrine falcon. There are mountain goats in the high places; and while bears now remain only in the place names, you might well hear the rustle of a wild boar in the woods. In l'Oisans you will certainly hear the shrill cry of the marmot, a large rodent something like the guinea-pig, and you may even be rewarded by a sighting in the woods, or on the high pastures of the Plateau d'Emparis. We even saw a mole, quite unperturbed by walkers, as it scuttled from one gallery to another in the sandy soil of the Bois de Claret.

But it is the flowers which attract the naturalist to the Dauphiné from early spring to late autumn. There is a variety of habitats; and the expert can gauge his height by the flora. Nothing can beat the pleasure of coming up through the woods into a high Alpine meadow studded with flowers – gentian, Alpine thistle, dwarf rhododendrons, orchids, corn flowers, martagon lily and orange lily. Even if you are not a botanist, take a flower book with you. If nothing else, flower identification will give you an opportunity to get your breath back!

Then there are the other walkers. The Dauphiné's large enough, and the paths are sufficiently numerous, for you to avoid other people altogether if you so wish. Even on the busiest summit you will never feel among a crowd. But you will meet walkers and, like walkers everywhere, they will be happy to stop for a chat – to tell you where they have come from, how long to the top, what other fine walks there are in the neighbourhood.

The villages of the Dauphiné are not the place to seek out the great triumphs of French architecture, and not all the modern building fits well into its surroundings. But there are nevertheless some little gems; and many of the details are delightful – tiny chapels and oratories perched on a knoll; the unmade streets of Les Terraces; the painted shutters on the house of Dr Lucher in La Grave; little hamlets clustered together of rough hewn stone, low eaves and wooden balconies, as often as not used for the storage of brushwood and *les blettes de fumier* – the peat-like fuel composed of dry sheep dung – against the bitter cold of winter.

And everywhere there are fountains. Some are no more than simple pipes gushing water into a horse trough, while others have elaborate spouts and elegantly arched surrounds. But whatever their architectural significance, they will be welcome during or after a hot day's walking. Mostly the water comes direct from a spring and is deliciously cool. Not even the champagne with which we celebrated the completion of our researches for this book could match the waters of the fountain of Gervais. And better still is the water of the source of the Romanche. Though that gushes direct from the living rock.

Walking in the Dauphiné offers many pleasures. There is no better way to get to know a country and its people – and the Dauphiné is well worth knowing. Many of the walks involve steep climbs, and at times you may think longingly of the fields of Kent or the marshes of Norfolk. But little can match the pleasure of climbing out of thick woods into the light and colour of a high Alpine meadow, with its vivid blues, purples and pinks, or of reaching a ridge and seeing, opening before you, range upon range of mountains into the distance and Mont Blanc raising its shoulders in the far north-east. Or of walking down an ancient green road into a hamlet, sitting at a table on the terrace of a little hotel, and calling for a carafe of wine and a tray of dominoes as the dusk thickens, the full moon rises over the shoulder of the mountain, and the lights begin to twinkle in the village far below.

How to Get There

Ferry and Train

The most convenient of the ferry ports serving France by boat and train for those travelling to Grenoble are:

Portsmouth – le Havre	P & O Ferries
Portsmouth – Caen	Brittany Ferries
Newhaven – Dieppe	Sealink
Dover/Ramsgate – Calais/Boulogne	Sealink/P & O Ferries
Dover – Boulogne	Hoverspeed

These may all be reached by rail from the main British towns.

Information on French railway services is available from major railway stations in the British Isles and from Gare SNCF de Grenoble, information 76 47 50 50 and booking office 76 47 54 27. There are frequent trains from the French ferry ports to Paris Gare du Nord or Gare de l'Est. Up to nine TGVs (*trains grande vitesse*) per day go direct to Grenoble from Paris Gare de Lyon – easily reached by metro or RER. The direct journey takes 3 hours 15 minutes for the 574km (357 miles). A further nine trains from the Gare de Lyon to Lyon Part-Dieu offer connections to Grenoble. Seat reservations must be secured for travel on the TGV; these cost FF13. It is possible to make reservations with automatic machines immediately before departure, but at holidays and busy times it is better to make reservations in advance. This may be done in major British railway stations and in all French stations.

SNCF (French railways) offer both 1st and 2nd class travel. There are reduced fares for young people and other categories of passenger; a full guide to train fares is provided in the French language *Guide Pratique du Voyageur*. It is more expensive to travel at certain times or on certain days; and on some of the TGVs a supplementary fare is required. (The cheapest fares are available on *Jours Bleus* (blue days); these are from Monday 12 noon to Friday 12 noon; Saturday 12 noon to Sunday 3pm; and some Bank Holiday mornings. On *Jours Blancs* (white days) some special reduced fares are not available; these cover Friday 12 noon to Saturday 12 noon, and Sunday 3pm to Monday 12 noon, and some Bank Holidays. *Jours Rouges* (red days) correspond to the main French holiday departure dates, such as the first weekends in July and August, and certain days at Christmas and Easter; no reduced fares are available on these dates.) A *Calendrier Voyageur*, available from any French railway station, gives details.

Frantour Tourisme offer special inclusive rates for train travel and hotel accommodation in Grenoble (and elsewhere); for information: French Railways Limited, 179 Piccadilly, London W1V OBA, Tel: 071 493 6594.

Motorail services are available from the UK and Ireland; information on motorail services in France is also available from French Railways Limited. Avis offers a package of train travel plus car hire, tel: 76 87 11 33.

Bicycles may be transported on French railways at a modest cost, but they are not accompanied by their owners and should be sent at least a day in advance. On certain short journeys bicycles may be taken free. Further details about these services are available from French Railways Limited.

Air

There are frequent air services to Paris from all the major British airports. Air France offers an inclusive fare for air and train travel to Grenoble (and other major French towns); information is readily available from travel agents. Tickets for this service must be booked two weeks in advance; in 1989 the return fare from London to Grenoble was £109, second class.

There are two regional airports offering frequent links with Grenoble. Grenoble Saint Geoirs is 30 minutes from Grenoble and offers connections to Paris (Air-Inter) and a fast shuttle service to Grenoble by bus (information 76 65 48 48). Lyon Satolas is one hour from Grenoble and offers connections to London and Paris; there is a frequent bus service to Grenoble (information 78 96 11 44).

Car

The quickest route to Grenoble from the channel ports is via Paris and the *autoroute du soleil* to Lyon. The journey is about 800km (500 miles). Allow about FF100 for motorway tolls (Visa is acceptable). There are numerous good restaurants on the route.

French motorways are generally two-lane and can get very congested, especially at the start of the French holidays, when pleasant alternative routes can be found. Unless otherwise indicated, the speed limit on motorways in France is 130kmph (80mph) and on other non-urban roads 90kmph (55mph). In towns the speed limit is 40kmph (25mph). There are frequent reminders by the roadside. The rule of the road is similar to that applying in Britain – with the crucial exceptions that the French drive on the right and that traffic coming from the right (ie the driver's near-side) generally has priority unless otherwise indicated. Watch out for signs indicating *Cédez le passage* (give way). The wearing of seatbelts by front seat passengers is compulsory.

Car drivers in France must be in possession of their national driving licence – British, other European Community, US, Australian and Canadian driving licences are acceptable. If using your own car, you require a Green Card for insurance, available from your own Insurance Company. Car hire is available at Grenoble Station and at major garages in the town.

Parking can be difficult in Grenoble; there are, however, a number of municipal car parks in the centre of the town and the number of spaces available in them is advertised on electronic notice-boards above many of the main roads into the town. Parking in the country towns does not in general present any difficulty.

Terrain and Climate

The Dauphiné contains four mountain ranges – la Chartreuse, le Vercors, le Massif de Belledonne and l'Oisans – and the broad glacial valley in which Grenoble is situated. All are within easy reach of Grenoble; the furthest villages of Haut Dauphiné (l'Oisans) and the southernmost part of le Vercors are only $1^{1}/_{2}$ hours' drive away. But, despite their proximity, there is considerable variety between, and indeed within them.

Le Vercors is the lowest range, rising to some 1,900m (6,230 ft) in the north and 2,300m (7,550ft) in the south. Because of the depth of its gorges and crevasses (*Gouffre Berger*), it has been said that le Vercors lies as much below ground as above. In the north, the hills are generally rounded and wooded and the valleys are broad and include excellent pastures. In the south, the spectacular limestone peak of Mont Aiguille rises sheer from the surrounding hills.

La Chartreuse – also limestone – is perhaps the most heavily wooded quarter. Its valleys are steeper than those of the northern Vercors and its summits are crowned with instantly recognisable peaks. The Désert de la Grande Chartreuse offers some of the most rewarding walking in the area; and the Alpine pastures of la Chartreuse are among the most colourful in the region.

Le Massif de Belledonne offers higher mountains still, much of them above the treeline. Walks here climb steeply over hard granite, leading to sombre mountain lakes and spectacular waterfalls. But the area offers charming lower level walks too; and the wooded lower valleys are reminiscent of Speyside.

L'Oisans, also of hard crystalline rocks and shales, has the highest peaks of the region, and is crowned by the eternal snows and the slowly moving glaciers of the High Alps. Even the valley floors are at 1,500m (5,000ft); and the Pic de la Meije rises to 3,982m (13,064ft). Here you will see the jagged peaks and immense cliffs which feature on every calendar in the region. But there are also surprises here – the grassy uplands of the Plateau d'Emparis which, despite its 2,000m (6,560ft) height, feels like the Scottish borders; and the hanging valley of the Plan des Alpes, high among glaciers, with its flat grasslands and meandering river.

The Dauphiné has a typical Alpine climate – very cold in winter, with a good deal of snow right down to the valley floors. Snow coverage is virtually guaranteed from 1,500m (5,000ft) from the end of November to mid-April (although in both 1988 and 1989 there was very little snow by Christmas), so not surprisingly, this is one of Europe's top skiing areas. Snows melt from the lower slopes in spring, giving way to a sea of snowdrops, daffodils and crocuses. March tends to be rainy, but April and May are fine and not too hot. Summer arrives at the end of May when the valleys can be uncomfortably hot; but it is possible to find cooler air in the mountains. L'Oisans is drier and hotter than the northern part of the region – and this is reflected in the flora, which tends to be more Mediterranean. The autumn inclines to be wet; and winter arrives, suddenly, in mid-November.

As always in the mountains the weather can change surprisingly fast. A sudden mountain storm can be an awesome – and sometimes a dangerous – experience; and they can happen at any time. Hope for the best; but be prepared for the worst. Weather forecasts may be readily obtained by phone (*Météo*; tel: 76 51 11 11) and many Syndicats d'Initiative post the local forecast outside their office. And it is always possible to seek local knowledge. As the *patronne* who served us in the café at la Tour Sans Venin told us, 'My husband listens to the forecast on the radio, but I know that when the top of that mountain (le Néron) has a cloud on it, it's going to be bad!'

Where to Stay

Accommodation for walkers in the Dauphiné does not pose any difficulties. A wide range of accommodation is available and hotels are surprisingly cheap by British and American standards; walkers are welcome and it is rarely necessary to book – though it is possible to make reservations through the local Syndicat d'Initiative. For those who wish to go back to nature, there are numerous campsites in the area, and *camping à la ferme* (pitching your tent on a farm or on someone's land) is increasingly popular, although there are restrictions in the National Parks and it is always advisable to seek permission.

Hotels in France are graded by stars, as in Britain, according to the facilities offered. Unlike in Britain, however, you pay for the room rather than the number of people. A room in a typical 2-star hotel costs in the order of FF120–180; in a 1-star FF100–150; and in a non-classified hotel upwards of FF80. The *Logis de France*, a national co-operative of small locally owned hotels, offer excellent value and service. Half pension and full pension terms are available in many hotels; half pension could cost of the order of FF140–200 per person (depending on the quality of the hotel); and full pension anything from FF180–250.

In the simpler non-classified hotels you might sit down to an excellent evening meal while, beyond a curtain, the proprietor's husband is putting his feet up in front of the television with a bottle of beer. In the more expensive hotels you will receive service unparalleled in Europe. And where else can you get an excellent dinner for two, palatable wines, accommodation, and a delightful view, for under £40?

Gîtes de France offer a variety of accommodation, ranging from holiday cottages (*le gîte rural*), and bed and breakfast (*la chambre (et la table) d'hôtes*) to simple hostels (*le gîte d'étape*), often on the routes of the Grandes Randonnées, or long distance footpaths. Information on such accommodation may be obtained from: Maison des Gites de France, 35 rue Godot-de-Mauroy, 75009 Paris, tel: 16 1 47 42 25 43. The cost of holiday cottages varies, according to size, facilities and season. Bed and breakfast costs about the same as a 1-star hotel – and again you pay by the room. Gîtes d'étapes are somewhat like youth hostels; they are cheaper than hotels – perhaps FF35–45 per person

– and they do offer a choice of both dormitories and small rooms.

Youth Hostels proper – *Auberges de la Jeunesse* – are rare in France outside the big cities, although there is a youth hostel in l'Alpe d'Huez. Unlike in England, and reflecting Cartesian logic, youth hostels in France are reserved for the young. Information on youth hostels in France may be obtained from the Youth Hostels Association, Trevelyan House, St Albans, Hertfordshire AL1 2DY.

Camping is popular, and there are a wide number and variety of campsites in the region. Campsites are graded according to facilities under a system of 1 to 5 stars; the cost varies according to the facilities provided. The more expensive might have a swimming pool, restaurant, shop, disco and hard standing for caravans. A typical 3-star campsite might cost around FF45–50 for two persons per night. *Camping à la ferme* offers a more primitive form of camping, and one which is more in keeping with the walker; facilities will be minimal – perhaps only a tap and a loo – but you will be closer to nature.

Cafés often offer accommodation at about the same cost as an unclassified hotel. Ask the proprietor.

Finally, there is a series of mountain huts or *abris*, many of which are run by the Club Alpin Français (some are reserved for members). Some have similar facilities to a gîte d'étape; others are no more than a shelter offering sleeping accommodation and sometimes a place to cook. *Abris* are marked on the 50,000 and 25,000 maps; further information may be obtained from: Club Alpin Français, 7 Rue de la Boétie, Paris 75008.

Getting about the Region

The easiest way to get about the Dauphiné is by car. It is possible to hire cars at many of the major garages in Grenoble – they will generally have a sign *'Location de Voitures'* – as well as at the railway station. Charges are similar to those applying in the UK. If you propose to hire a car, remember to take your driving licence with you.

None of the areas described in this book is more than about $1\frac{1}{2}$ hours' drive from Grenoble. The main roads out of the town are good and traffic jams are unusual. There are, however, very few lengths of dual carriageway and overtaking can be difficult, particularly in the mountains. Side roads are generally well graded and pose no undue difficulty for the driver. The only difficult drive associated with the walks in this book is that to the Plateau d'Emparis – Walk 26 – which involves a steep climb up hairpins on an unmade road. In general, however, driving in the region is a pleasure.

You may wish to hire a bicycle to approach the start of some of the walks, or even to do them! There are facilities for the hire of mountain bikes – VTT (*vélos tous terrains*) – in many of the villages and resorts in the region. Charges range from about FF50–100 per day. Try Mountain Bike Diffusion, 6 quai de France, 38000 Grenoble, tel: 76 47 58 76 to hire VTT; they also arrange excursions in which you can leave Grenoble by bus and return by mountain bike. Bicycles are also available from Borel Sport, 42 rue Alsace-Lorraine, tel: 76 46 47 46.

Some *téléphériques* (cablecars) work in summer; the service from Grenoble to the Bastille is useful to approach the start of Walk 2; and the service from Huez to Alpe d'Huez and from Alpe d'Huez to Lac Blanc for the start of Walk 24.

It is possible to approach many of the walks in this book by public transport, although a longer walk may be involved to reach the start of the walk, and care will be required to ensure that the walk plus any extension can be done in the time available. Timetables vary according to winter and summer seasons and whether or not the schools are in session, so it is essential to seek advice. Advice and timetables are available from Grenoble railway station (*gare SNCF*) (tel: 76 47 50 50) and bus station (*gare routière*) (tel: 76 47 77 77), which are beside each other in the Place de la Gare.

The most useful bus services for approaching the walks described in this book are provided by the VFD and leave from the *gare routière*. The following are the principal services serving the areas of the walks:

Vercors	VFD Service 510
Chartreuse	VFD Service 714
	Cars de Chartreuse (tel: 76 50 81 18)
Belledonne	VFD Service 601
	Brun Autocars (tel: 76 09 64 27)
Oisans	VFD Services 302 and 306.

Further details are given in Appendix 2.

Taxis are available in Grenoble and in many of the surrounding towns and villages. Details of taxi firms are available from local Syndicats d'Initiative.

Money

Currency is the French franc (FF), worth, in 1990, about FF9.20 to the £ sterling. Money may be changed in most – but not all – of the banks in the region, who will also change travellers' cheques and Eurocheques. If you need to take large sums abroad it will be convenient to take travellers' cheques or to arrange with your bank to draw on your own account by means of Eurocheques. Make sure that you are not caught out by Bank Holidays.

The major credit cards – Visa, Access, American Express – are accepted in most larger shops, hotels and restaurants, who will also accept payment in Eurocheques. Certain credit cards – eg Visa – may also be used to draw money from the money dispensers of the Crédit Lyonnais and the Banque Rhône Alpes, the two major banks of the region. Some garages accept credit cards, particularly those on the motorways and main roads; but in country districts it may be necessary to use cash to buy petrol. Small shops and hotels also tend to deal in cash.

The Law for the Walker

The legal system of France is related to that of Scotland; and the approach to walkers in both countries is broadly similar. In brief, you can go virtually anywhere on paths or tracks, provided that you do not damage crops or endanger livestock. Many paths pass close to, or even through, farmyards or the gardens of country retreats; here you are likely to be greeted with a smile and an offer of local information or directions.

But privileges involve responsibilities. There is no French Country Code as such (code in France implies something of legal authority; and a voluntary code could not be enforced). Always follow these principles:

Leave gates as you find them
Do not damage or destroy anything
Take all your litter back with you
Do not uproot or pick plants or flowers
Do not disturb wildlife
Protect the environment
Wherever possible, stay on footpaths
Do not make fires or smoke in forests
Do not make unnecessary noise
Enjoy yourself and permit others to do likewise

The Dauphiné has local laws against gathering snails; and you will see notices warning *'Rammassage des Escargots Interdit sous Peine de Procès Verbal'* (gathering snails forbidden; offenders will be prosecuted). Walnuts are also a valuable crop, and collecting them is theft. But you may freely gather the wild raspberries, strawberries and bilberries growing on the hillsides.

In the Parc National des Ecrins (Oisans) camping and camp fires are forbidden; however if you are more than 2 hours from the boundaries of the Park you are permitted to bivouac for one night. Elsewhere, *camping à la ferme* is permitted (*see* 'Where to Stay' on p.13); but you should always seek local advice.

If you run into any serious difficulty, contact your nearest Consul. Their addresses are given in Appendix 1.

Clothing and Equipment

The walks in this book have been designed for walking when the snow is off the ground; in winter the Dauphiné is more suitable for skiing than for walking. (If, however, you wish to attempt any of the walks when there *is* snow on the ground, do take advice on equipment.) None of the walks involves rock-climbing (although there are one or two steep scrambles) or glacier walking, so ropes, crampons, pitons and ice-axes are not required. Whenever you walk, stout walking boots, warm clothing, waterproofs, gloves and a hat are essential.

The first essentials you require are map and compass (*see* 'Navigation' on p.23). Next in importance is footwear. Many of the paths described can be slippery in wet weather and the shale of the High Dauphiné is particularly treacherous. Boots with a good grip are therefore essential; trainers give insufficient grip and insufficient support to the ankles. In generally dry weather lightweight fell boots will suffice; indeed, all the walks described in this book were done in such boots. But in wet weather, and over the more rocky paths – Grand Som, Lac de Crop, Cascade de l'Oursière, Lac Blanc and the source of the Romanche – leather walking boots would be preferable; and in spring and autumn they are essential.

As to clothing, in high summer shorts and a T-shirt will often suffice on the lower slopes. But it is essential to carry a warm sweater and waterproof clothing and useful to have a change of socks. A hat and good polaroid or UV sunglasses are also desirable.

It is important to wear bright colours; and rucksacks and anoraks nowadays can be very eyecatching. A water bottle is essential; and in summer you will drink far more than in Britain. Water is available on most of the walks – the Vercors is the exception – so a litre bottle should be enough. Mineral water bottles provide a light alternative to the usual plastic bottle.

You will need a rucksack to carry waterproofs, water, a picnic and spare clothing. Rucksacks are available in a great variety of shapes and sizes, but you will not require anything too big for a day's hike. Comfort and convenience are the criteria: avoid frames; seek padded straps; and choose a rucksack with a number of side pockets, so that you can have ready access to small items without having to unpack. One of your party should carry a first-aid kit (*see* 'Health Hazards' on p.22).

You will have your own views on photography; but 125 and Instamatic cameras are almost useless in the mountains. A good 35mm camera is ideal. Miniature 35mm are light and produce excellent results. Binoculars are useful, both to look at birds and animals, and in some cases to spy out the land – 8 x 30 are light and have a usefully wide field of view.

Finally, you will require a stick, both to help you climb, and to ward off dogs, vipers and Italian mountain bikers! It is possible to buy sticks, decorated with eidelweiss and the names of resorts, for about FF30–50. But you can find one in the first forest that you enter; make sure that it will not snap at your weight. After a week or two's walking in the mountains, it will have become a real friend.

Food and Wine

Walking gives one a healthy appetite, and the Dauphiné allows ample opportunity to indulge it. Breakfast (not usually included in the price of an hotel room) will consist of black or milky coffee (*café noir* or *café crème*) with croissants or *tartines* (crusty French bread and butter), which can be purchased at the bar. Most places also do *petit déjeûner complet* for about FF15, comprising the above with jam or honey as well.

A packed lunch is the best idea if you are planning to spend the whole day walking. There is a *boulangerie* in every tiny village where you can purchase rolls, *baguettes* or even sliced bread (of a better variety than in Britain, mostly used for posh cocktail parties). The local *épicerie* (for cheeses, fruit, milk produce, chocolate) and *charcuterie* (for sliced sausage (*saucisson*), ham or pâté) will provide the rest of the picnic and will see you through until evening and the wild call of the *apéritif.*

Saucisson comes in several forms: the dry variety (*saucisson sec*) which is probably the best for hikers in that it can be hacked at any point of the walk and will keep practically for ever, and the sliced variety – of perhaps a more refined taste – which you buy and eat on the same day. Try 'Jésus' variety – one of the best saucisson of the region. This is eaten in thin slices and is available in any *charcuterie*. For the best food value for weight try *la viande des Grisons*, produced by drying ham in the rafters and originating from the Swiss region of the same name. Such a packed lunch will cost approximately FF15 per person. Sandwiches (*casse-croute*) are available ready-made from any café. The sign *hors sac* means that you can consume your own food on the premises. You are, however, expected to buy a drink!

Cheeses – as in all parts of France – are plentiful and there are some local specialities which must be sampled. They come in two forms: *fromage cuit* – like Gruyère, Cantal, Tome de Savoie – which can be purchased by weight, and *tomes* – small round dry cheeses made of raw cow's or goat's milk – which are purchased *à la pièce*. St Marcellin is one of the best known of the region and is sold either fresh (soft and white) or dry (yellow). It is the traditional shepherds' food; it can be kept in your rucksack for days and only improves with age. Villagers will also sell you their own brands of *tomes* and these are possibly the best and cheapest – *see* Walks 13 and 14 (Charmant Som) and Walk 7 (la Balme de Rencurel). However, best of all is indubitably the *fromage blanc* – the Dauphinois dessert *par excellence*. It is made of the curd of cow's milk and is served in all restaurants, from the most modest to the most epicurian, on a bed of fresh cream sprinkled with caster sugar.

If all this has not yet spoilt your appetite, then you are ready for the event which will make all the cols and dales worthwhile – *le dîner*. You will find mouth-watering menus in places ranging from cafés (*bistros*) to 3-star hotel restaurants. But do not leave it too late – most places stop serving by 9.30pm. Most restaurants offer a range of menus varying from FF50 to FF150 according to the number of dishes and the quality of the food. You may wish to conclude your walks with a *menu gastronomique*, as we did; but most menus offer food of excellent quality, often with a distinctive local flavour. Try the *salade montagnarde* (green salad with walnuts, gruyère, bacon and *vinaigrette*), *fondue savoyarde* (cheese fondue), the excellent steaks and the *tartes à la noix*. Excellent local cuisine may also be had in many of the region's refuges; at the Refuge du Fay in the Plateau d'Emparis (Walk 26) we dined handsomely off vegetable soup in which whole vegetables swam and a local delicacy – belly of pork with dumplings made of Alpine herbs according to a closely guarded secret recipe; followed, of course, by locally produced *fromage blanc*.

But the prince of the region's cuisine is *gratin Dauphinois*. To say that it is made of thinly sliced potatoes belies its nobility and its delicacy. It may be found in the simplest café, where it provides a welcome meal after a winter walk, or the 3-star restaurant, where it provides the accompaniment to other dishes which may be more grandiose but are no more delicious. Its mastery takes a long apprenticeship but we have included the recipe in Appendix 3.

Apart from the milk which forms the basis for its marvellous cheeses, the Dauphiné is famous the world over for its walnuts. These are used in a variety of foods, the most important being the *noix de Grenoble*, a confectionery made from chocolate or marzipan and walnuts, shaped like a walnut. (These could make an ideal present for those who have cared for your animals during your tour.) *Pâtissiers* compete against each other for the most original walnut cakes; the hunt is up to you.

Although you will see vineyards on the lower slopes of the Dauphiné, no great vintages are produced here. The Dauphinois call the local wine *une piquette* (a rough and ready brew); but it can form a pleasant accompaniment to a lunchtime sandwich if you do not propose to walk too far in the afternoon. The region's main claims to fame in the field of drink are first the liqueurs produced by the monks of the Chartreuse (Walks 15 and 16), although these are no longer produced at the monastery but in the nearby town of Voiron, and secondly the Vin de Noix, a walnut wine made in September, usually *à la ferme*, from the Dauphiné's most celebrated crop. Vin de Noix is best drunk young and it is usually ready by Christmas. The other regional speciality is Suze – a cordial distilled from gentian flowers – and it is an acquired taste: to my palate it has a bouquet like the sap of daffodils and a bitter aftertaste. But, if you walk in the region in summer and see the headless stalks of gentians everywhere you go, you may wish to try it and become legless on the results.

Excellent wines are to be found in most restaurants and hotels; and many specialise in the wines of the neighbouring province of Savoie, which produces excellent dry whites and light and fruity rosés and red wines, as well as the more substantial Mondeuse. The dry whites are particularly suitable for drinking with Dauphinois cheeses; Johnson and Duijker (*Wine Atlas of France*) liken them to 'bottled mountain air'. The wines of the district of Crépy are bottled *sur lie*, leaving them slightly sparkling. La Roussette, also known as Altesse, is one of the best known white wines of the region, and is the traditional accompaniment to *fondue Savoyarde*.

At the other extremity of the region, in the southernmost part of the Vercors, lies the town of Die, famous for its white *vin mousseux*, made according to the *méthode Champenoise*, and known as *la Clairette de Die*. It is a noble rival to champagne.

Wherever you go, local people will be happy to discuss the local wines and to engage in abstruse debates about the quality of the vintage: you may not even be aware that this is the subject of discussion! We were given a bottle of Chateauneuf du Pape 1986 by a rather inebriated shepherd in the Plateau d'Emparis (Walk 26), simply because we had been practising French numerals!

Preparations for the Voyage

Documentation

Visas are not required by nationals of the European Community or Switzerland. Non European Community nationals should obtain a visa from any French consulate before departure as visas are *not* issued on arrival at a French port or airport. The addresses of French consulates in Britain, the US, Canada, and Australia are given in Appendix I.

European Community nationals holding national passports (or a British Visitor's Passport) may stay in France for up to 90 days. Those wishing to stay longer should apply to a police station for a *Carte de Séjour*.

British nationals wishing to take advantage of the reciprocal arrangements for payment of medical costs (*see* 'Health Hazards' on p.22) should apply to their local Post Office for Form E111 before departure. Others should check their personal health insurance. There are no specific vaccination requirements for those wishing to enter France.

Those wishing to take their own car to France should arrange with their insurance company for the issue of a Green Card, and should adjust their headlamps to comply with French regulations (*see* also 'How to Get There' on p.9). Further advice is available from the Automobile Association.

Checklist of documentation

Passport
Visa (for non EC nationals)
Travel tickets
Form E111 (for British nationals) or Health Insurance
Driving licence
Green Card (for motor insurance)
Travellers' Cheques or Eurocheques, plus credit cards and currency

Other Preparations

Those wishing to undertake detailed planning of their walks in advance may wish to purchase the appropriate maps. IGN maps are available, in Britain, from E Stanford of Longacre, London, and from many good bookshops and specialist sports shops. They are also readily available from bookshops in Grenoble and from Maison de la Randonnée, CIMES-GTA, 7 rue Voltaire, 38000 Grenoble, Tel: 76 51 76 00.

Health Hazards

Walking in the Dauphiné is unlikely to cause any damage to your health if you take reasonable care. In summer it is essential to guard against sunstroke and sunburn; wear a cotton hat and, if you have a sensitive skin, an ultra-violet screener. In winter there is a risk of frostbite – although none of the walks in this book is designed for winter walking; dress warmly and ensure that extremities are kept warm.

Many books on the Alps recommend that you carry an anti-snakebite serum although the chances of being bitten are slight. Alpine vipers are as shy as adders – and the side-effects of the serum can be harmful, as can the application of a tourniquet. It is possible to purchase for about FF79 at any good pharmacy a syringe for drawing out venom – *Aspivenin*. This is very light; it sucks out about 60 per cent of the venom by creating a vacuum around the affected area if it is held in place for at least 40 seconds. It is imperative to consult a doctor as soon as possible after a snakebite. The poisonous Alpine viper – *la vipère* – is relatively stumpy and of a reddish-brown colour with a lozenge-shaped head, linear pupils and three parallel bars running down its forehead between the eyes. It is not to be confused with a harmless greenish snake – *la couleuvre* – which is longer and has round pupils and a very scaly hide. The best remedy against snakes is to carry a walking stick, but you are most unlikely to be troubled with them.

There are few problems with insects, although wasps (*guêpes*) abound in summer. The *Aspivenin* may also be used to deal with wasp stings and insect bites.

Rabies – *la rage* – is endemic in the Dauphiné; dogs and cats should be treated with caution. Any dog or cat bite should receive *immediate* medical attention. Tetanus is also endemic; deep cuts should receive medical attention, especially if you have not recently been vaccinated against tetanus.

There is always the possibility of an accident when walking in the hills, although none of the walks described here is dangerous. One of your party should carry a first aid kit (*trousse de secours*) containing plasters, bandages, antiseptics and pain reliever. In spring and autumn it is also desirable to carry a survival bag. Pharmacies, to be found in all towns and most villages, will give first aid treatment for a small fee.

In case of emergency, police, ambulance and mountain rescue (*Secours en Montagne*) may be contacted by dialling 17. Charges are levied for calling out the mountain rescue services although it is possible to insure against these eventualities.

Nationals of the European Community may receive assistance towards the cost of medical treatment in France: the State meets 80 per cent of hospital fees and 75 per cent of other medical costs. British citizens should obtain Form E111 from their local Post Office before leaving for France to enable them to benefit from these arrangements. Hospital fees are sorted out by the hospital authorities; in due course you will receive a bill for 20 per cent of the cost. Other medical consultations are charged at the time of the visit – the cost of a consultation is of the order of FF100. The patient is presented with a certificate (the *feuille de soins*) indicating the charges. Prescriptions are also paid for at the time of receipt. A sticky label on the medicine container should be affixed to the *feuille de soins* as proof of payment. At the end of your visit send the *feuille de soins* to the local office of the Caisse Primaire, together with the form E111; in due course you will be refunded 75 per cent of admissible costs. Any doctor or pharmacist providing treatment will advise on the address of the nearest Caisse Primaire.

Alternatively, you may prefer to take out health insurance. This may be readily secured through travel agents, or your usual insurance company.

Navigation in the Mountains

Map and compass are essential items of equipment for anyone walking in the French Alps, even on well waymarked paths. The 1:50,000 maps (broadly equivalent to the OS maps of the same scale) published by Didier and Richard for the Institut Géographique National (IGN) in the series *Cartes et Guides Touristiques* identify the main footpaths and are useful for general planning; the relevant maps for the Dauphiné are:

4   Chartreuse – Belledonne – Maurienne
6   Massif des Ecrins – Haut Dauphiné
12   Massif du Vercors

But, scale for scale, the French maps include less detail than the British; and the 1:50,000 series is not detailed enough for close navigation on the ground. For this the 1:25,000 *Blue Series* published by the IGN is essential. The relevant map is indicated at the beginning of the description of each walk. Even these maps contain less information than the British 1:25,000 map, particularly of forest tracks, although the Grande Randonnée (GR) paths are clearly indicated. A compass is absolutely essential, and the walker should never depart without one. Best is a properly damped compass which can be used to take bearings, such as is produced by SILVA or Suunto.

Many paths are waymarked but there are also other marks in forests and it is important not to confuse them. With their passion for standardisation, the French have made it easy for the walker. Footpaths are indicated as follows:

two horizontal bars, red over white

waymarked national long-distance footpath (*sentier de Grande Randonnée*)

two horizontal bars, red over yellow

waymarked local footpath (*GR de pays*)

orange bar or disc

bridleway

diagonal cross (in colours of waymarks)

no road – do not follow this path

Unexpected changes of direction in a GR are indicated by a waymark in the appropriate colours forming an angle showing the new direction of the path. Waymarks can appear on any permanent object – treetrunks, large stones or rocks, fence posts, lamp-posts and so on. On rocks, paths are sometimes indicated by a white, red or blue circle, bar or lozenge. On some walks there are signposts; these will often give a colour coding for a particular path.

In forests, horizontal red bars (sometimes superimposed on white) indicate the limits of a parcel of woodland and are associated with painted signs giving letters or numbers. They are *not* waymarks. In the Parc Naturel Régional du Vercors are a large number of walks marked not simply by the horizontal bars described above, but also by a gentian sign and a specific number. In the walk descriptions these are referred to as Gentian Waymark 1 or Gentian Waymark 54, as the case may be. *Carto-guides* to these walks may be obtained from Maison du Parc, Chemin des Fusillés, Lans-en-Vercors, BP 14, 38250, Villard-de-Lans, tel: 76 95 40 33, or from local Syndicats d'Initiative (tourist offices).

Walking in mountains can take far longer than over the equivalent distance of flat or rolling terrain; and it can take almost as long to descend as to ascend. It can, in particular, take a deceptively long time to descend on hairpins (*lacets*) through forests. Take care not to overestimate the distance you have covered in such circumstances.

Place names give a good deal of information about terrain, but their significance is not always clear even to native speakers. In Appendix 4 we give a list of some of the more common topographical terms which you find on maps of the area.

The walks in this book are classified according to difficulty into Easy (1) or (2), Moderate (3) or (4), Difficult (5) or (6). A walk classified as Easy (1) will be generally on the level, although perhaps with some gentle gradients; it should be well within the capabilities of any moderately fit walker. Easy (2) has rather more in the way of gradients. Moderate walks involve more climbing; those classified Moderate (4) are generally longer and require more stamina. Difficult walks should be attempted only by the experienced and fit; those classified Difficult (6) are long and challenging and may involve some scrambling.

The times indicated in the walk summaries are the times likely to be taken by relatively fit walkers who are not overexerting themselves and allow for picnic breaks, breaks to look at the view, and breaks simply to get your breath back. They are nevertheless shorter than most of the times indicated on signposts in the area. If in doubt, give yourself longer to finish the walk, particularly if you propose to walk in the late afternoon.

THE WALKS

Walk 1   The Bastille and the Grottes de Mandrin

Map no	IGN 3234 est
Distance	5km (3 miles)
Ascent	300m (984ft)
Walking time	$2^1/_2$ hours
Grading	Easy (2)

This is an easy walk of some 5km, offering a climb of almost 300m (984ft) from 213m to 498m (699ft to 1,634ft). For the experienced walker it may seem rather tame; but from the top there are extensive views of Grenoble and of the main mountain ranges visited by the other walks described in this book, so it provides a useful means of orientation. Those who wish to preserve their strength for the later walks may wish to take the *Téléphérique* (cablecar) from the banks of the Isère (FF16, 50; service from 9am (11am on Mondays) to 12.30am).

The Walk

The walk starts near the town centre, by the banks of the River Isère near the foot of the *Téléphérique*. It is possible to park near here. Walk upstream along the Quai Stéphane Jay towards an elegant wrought iron footbridge, the Pont St Laurent. In the distance upstream can be seen Chamechaude and Mont Rachais in the Chartreuse range, and on the far bank of the river is the Quartier St Laurent, formerly derelict, but now elegantly restored.

Pass over the Pont St Laurent to the right bank of the river, noting the

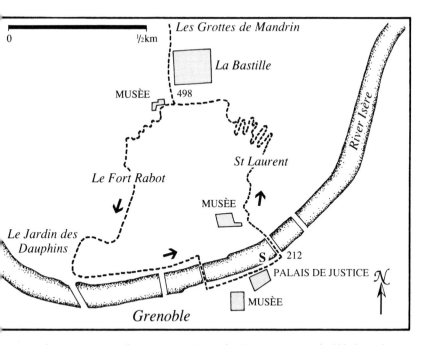

Les Grottes de Mandrin

La Bastille

MUSÈE 498

Le Fort Rabot

St Laurent

MUSÈE

Le Jardin des
Dauphins

S 212

PALAIS DE JUSTICE

MUSÈE

Grenoble

River Isère

0 ½km

N

views downstream to the Vercors. Cross the Quai Mounier half left to the Place Cymaise. The monument facing you features the emblem of Grenoble – a lion fighting with a snake – flanked by dolphins and surmounted by three roses. It commemorates a visit by the Roman Proconsul Lucius Munatius Plancus in 43BC. Plancus describes, in a letter to Cicero, how he gave Grenoble the name of Cularo Verso and built the first bridge across the Isère; this was on the site of the Pont St Laurent and was subsequently replaced by the mediaeval Pont de Bois, which was then the only bridge across the Isère.

From the monument climb the steps of the Montée de Chalemond; a signpost points to the 'Téléphérique Accès pour Piétons' and the Musée Dauphinois, which has a fine collection of general and regional interest. The steps up the hill are cobbled and flanked by high walls, part of the defences constructed by Vauban, Louis XIV's Minister of Defence. As you climb note the views to the east across the town to the Massif de Belledonne (see Walks 17 to 22), and the contrast between the pantiles of the old town and the concrete of the high-rise flats of Grenoble's post-war expansion.

The path passes through a wooden gate and turns right at the end of the wall; from here it ascends steeply between an immense wall and shady trees. Where it meets a broader track there is a signpost to the Téléphérique; follow this up the hill ahead of you (the path to the left goes to the Musée

Dauphinois and the path downhill to the Church of St Laurent, again well worth a visit). When you reach the base of further fortifications, follow the main path round to the left, keeping the wall on your right. Turn past the floodlighting, ignoring the path up under the cliffs marked *Sans Issue* (no way out), and climb the steps on the right (marked by a blue arrow) through a steep passage in the fortifications (the shade in summer will be most welcome!). As you leave the tunnel a white arrow on the ground leads you round past some iron railings to an oak door studded with iron nails, and up further steps. At the signpost ascend the stairs to the right and follow the blue arrows up the hill, pausing a moment to look down at the gravelled cemeteries on either bank of the Isère. There are faded notices on the walls signposted to the *Téléphérique*, leading after a short distance to the summit.

Here, at 498m, is the Restaurant du Téléphérique, which is not cheap, but there are marvellous views. On the terrace above is a *Table d'Orientation*.

Past the head of the *Téléphérique* a path leads up the hill towards the Grotte de Mandrin. Mandrin was the Robin Hood or Dick Turpin of French legend and not surprisingly the Grotte has nothing whatever to do with him. Another restaurant – Chez le Per' Gras – is at the head of the path; and from here start a number of walks, including that to the Mont du Rachais (Walk 2), the Mont Jalla and St Martin le Vinoux, and the Croix de Montfleury. The grottes, which are in the cliff-face to the left of the path, are normally illuminated from 1 April to 30 September from 6am to 9pm, and from 1 October to 31 March from 7am to 7pm; if not, it is possible to buy torches in the shop at the head of the *Téléphérique*. A notice summarises the history of the caves; roughly translated, it reads: 'So called Mandrin's Cave, excavated in 1844 by the army. These openings in the rock were equipped with five guns able to beat off an enemy advancing on the fort. The tunnel was built a few years later. It allowed the soldiers stationed in the cave to regain the fort out of sight of the enemy.' From the caves it is possible to regain the head of the téléphérique through the tunnel, and along a mule track – le Sentier des Muletiers – running along the side of the cliff.

Follow the signpost downhill towards the Sortie des Dauphins (which closes at 7.30pm in summer) and le Parc Guy Pape. On the left is the Fort du Rabot, a military barracks built to look like a fourteenth century castle. Halfway down the hill the path forks. Follow the signposts to the Jardin des Dauphins under the wall of the Fort du Rabot and over a metal bridge; here, after a steep descent through a tunnel, are the gardens. An elegant cast iron drinking fountain greets you as you enter. Further down, and through another short tunnel, is a café – the Chalet des Dauphins – which sells fine ice-creams and *crêpes au chocolat* (FF14). Notice the cannon-ball cemented into the wall

The battlements, La Bastille

as you emerge from the tunnel. Below to the left is a children's play park, and further down still as you approach the road an equestrian statue of the Dauphinois heroine Philis de la Charce (1645–1703). Follow the Quai de France upstream, past the school and the fine modern building of the Crédit Immobilier de Grenoble, and cross the river by the Pont Marius Gontard opposite the Le Mandrin Grill. From here it is an easy step back to the foot of the *Téléphérique*.

Walk 2 Mont Rachais

Map no	IGN 3234 est
Distance	5$\frac{1}{2}$km (3$\frac{1}{2}$ miles)
Ascent	564m (1,800ft)
Walking time	3 hours
Grading	Easy (2); difficult alternative descent (5)

This is an easy walk to the summit of the mountain behind La Bastille at 1,046m (3,432ft), and gives wide views over the city of Grenoble and the hills of la Chartreuse. It has a difficult alternative descent which might be suitable for those who wish to prepare for some of the more strenuous walks elsewhere in the region.

Take the steep minor road leading to the Site de La Bastille from D512 to la Tronche on the right bank of the Isère; alternatively, take the *Téléphérique* from Grenoble to the Bastille and make your way to the start of the walk from there. There is a large car park by the Restaurant Chez le Per' Gras.

The Walk

The walk to the Balcon du Rachais (marked with green waymarks) leads off to the left of the restaurant by the signpost and climbs the hill northwards behind it, initially on the route of GR9 which is marked by red and white waymarks. The track is of grey gravel; there are views over the more affluent quarters of Grenoble and the villages on the flanks of Mont St Eynard on whose summit, at the top of spectacular cliffs, is the Fort du St Eynard. The path heads northwards through an ancient oak forest; the town becomes rapidly hidden but its presence is still felt from the sound of traffic.

After a few hundred metres the path takes a sharp hairpin; follow the signpost to the Col de Cuigne. The signpost has a number of waymarks, including the red and white of the GR9 and the green of the Balcon du Rachais. Follow the hairpins up the hill on a very well-made path, leaving the noise of traffic behind as you climb. A path leads off to the left, marked with a red and white diagonal cross; such marks indicate that the waymarked path

31

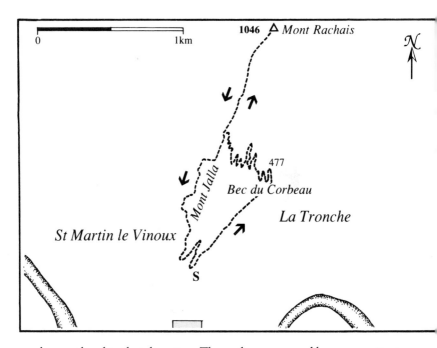

does *not* head in that direction. The path narrows and becomes quite steep, climbing the right-hand flank of the hill and marked by red and white and green waymarks on boulders.

After a climb of some 35 to 40 minutes the path levels off and turns sharp right; there is a red and white waymark on a tree to the left of the track. The path crosses a shoulder and turns sharp left up the hill to overlook Grenoble. The trees begin to thin, and there is a profusion of wild flowers among grasses. Twenty minutes further on the trees thin out considerably and the ground falls steeply away to the right; it is possible to see from here how flat the glacial floor of the valley is.

The path broadens and passes a house on the right-hand side. 200m beyond the house a path turns sharply uphill back to the left; the main path continues northwards; and another path heads downhill to La Tronche and la Vièrge Noire – the Black Virgin – who is well worth a visit if you do not wish to ascend the hill. Housed in a neatly restored chapel, she is an elegant representative of a cult which was widespread in this part of Europe in the Middle Ages and her shrine is garlanded with flowers and contains many votive offerings.

But to ascend the hill take the sharp left turn; a wooden arrow nailed to a tree above the path marks its direction. From this point the meanders of the

Grenoble from la Vierge Noire

Isère are clearly discernible and, depressingly close, the car park by Chez le Per' Gras where the walk began.

The path leads diagonally up through meadows with a wealth of wild flowers, including wild carnations; crickets bask on the rocks. It re-enters the wood and climbs westwards towards a saddle on the summit ridge. At the ridge turn right and walk northwards through trees and shrub. There are steep cliffs to the right; the path becomes very rocky and, in places, requires scrambling. It is clearly marked with red waymarks to which it is essential to keep. The summit is marked by a rusty metal pole on which are painted two red marks.

From the summit there are superb views northwards to the Massif de la Chartreuse, and to the cliffs of le Néron to the west and the Fort du St Eynard to the east. On a good day it is possible to see Mont Blanc to the far NE. To the south Le Moucherotte is clearly identifiable in the Vercors.

From the summit retrace your steps to the saddle. From here it is possible to retrace your tracks, or to take a far more difficult descent which is signposted, from the saddle, to Mont Jalla. This path continues along the ridge for a short distance, then turns right downhill, initially somewhat overgrown and then through a grassy clearing from which there are wide views of the city. The path, marked by parallel red marks on the trees, descends steeply through young oaks, heading in the direction of Le Moucherotte. Immediately below is the Bastille and the car park at the start of the walk; and running through the city away from you the Cours de la Libération, which heads south to the Mediterranean. The path continues down a steep cliff, definitely not for softies and requiring some scrambling and great care, and then steeply past a large boulder, marked with a double red waymark, until it rejoins the track that you took on your ascent. Follow this down to the start of the walk.

An alternative descent would be to retrace your steps from the saddle to the point at which the path to the summit turns sharp left uphill (marked by the wooden arrow nailed on a tree). From here a path leads downhill to La Vièrge Noire above La Tronche. From La Tronche is a frequent bus service into Grenoble.

Walk 3   Tour Sans Venin and St Nizier

Map no	IGN 3235 ouest
Distance	7.5km (4.7 miles)
Ascent	570m (1,870ft)
Walking time	3 hours
Grading	Moderate (3)

This is a moderate walk of 7.5km, much of it through attractive woodlands, which gives fine views of the spectacular limestone pinnacles at the north eastern extremity of the Vercors, Les Trois Pucelles (the Three Maidens), and an opportunity to visit the pleasant Alpine resort of St Nizier du Moucherotte. Those who wish to extend the walk may climb Le Moucherotte from St Nizier (*see* Walk 3A).

Take the D106 Seyssins and St Nizier road from Grenoble to Tour Sans Venin. The castle after which the hamlet is named is on a knoll on the right-hand side of the road; on a fine summer's day it looks as peaceful as its name (the Tower without Venom) suggests.

The Walk

The walk begins on the rue de l'Ecole, which leads sharply uphill to the left by a pedestrian crossing and bus stop immediately opposite the Restaurant Bar Au Bon Coin. (Parking is possible near the restaurant, or opposite the Restaurant Bouchet which is just before the Bon Coin.) The first half of the walk follows the GR9 E4, and is clearly waymarked with white and red parallel bars.

The track passes a farm on the right, and a house with brown shutters beside a ruinous barn on the left. After a sharp climb it reaches a road; to the right can be seen the buildings of a disused railway station. (French provincial stations were all built to the same design and are unmistakable.) The path leads uphill NW behind the station; it is clearly waymarked on the concrete powerline posts and on a metal plate to the left. The path takes a sharp bend through a cutting in the rocks and approaches a meadow on the left-hand

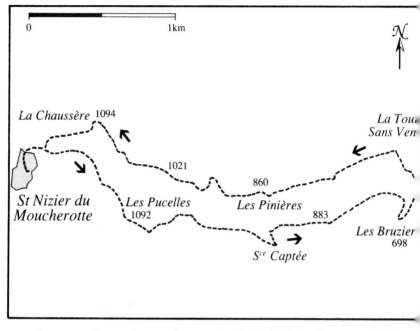

side. Across the meadow can be seen the cliffs of Le Moucherotte and below them the woods through which you will return.

Continue climbing up a moderate gradient through a mixed wood of oak and beech, following clearly defined waymarks. The path passes under powerlines and leads uphill westwards directly towards Les Trois Pucelles. It joins a wider gravelled track by an electricity substation and continues westwards with woods on the left and steeply falling meadows to the right. Note the dressed stone block with the number 14 carved on it on the right-hand side of the track; this marks the boundary of a parcel of forest. Below on the right can be seen the D106 snaking up the hillside in hairpins, and the pantiled roof of an old barn. The track leads gently up the hill to the house of Les Pinières and joins the D106 at 860m (2,822ft) after a climb of some 45 minutes.

A short way up the road a track leads off half left, marked by a waymark on a concrete power post. Follow this uphill directly towards les Trois Pucelles, passing to the right of an electricity substation. Turn right where the track meets a T-junction and follow the path as it snakes up the hill. At the first junction after the T-junction turn left uphill to reach a gate with a chain across the road and a notice 'Propriété Privée: Défense d'Entrer'. Here the path turns right, passing a house to the left. A notice warns you that it is forbidden

36

The church at St Nizier

to pick flowers or to collect snails. Cross the little cart track which leads left to Les Michalons and continue straight on up the hill half right to reach some powerlines on a metalled road; to the left is a fine view of Les Trois Pucelles. Follow the metalled road past some pine trees until you reach concrete gateposts; here turn left up a path marked by a red-topped post. The path, which is likely to be very wet in rainy weather, climbs steadily under large trees, passing a modern house to the left and crossing a metalled road and then a track (after which the gradient slackens) to reach a hayfield on the right. There are views from here eastwards to the Néron and the Dent de Crolles in the Chartreuse.

Cross the D106 half left, following the little road marked by a double waymark and a signpost to La Chaussère uphill NW; in the right foreground is a French *tricolore* marking the monument to the Resistance of the Vercors. (This area was noted for the strength of the resistance offered by the *Maquis*.) Beyond are views to the Massif de la Chartreuse. The road bends sharply to the left towards a steep roofed chalet; on the right is a farmyard, beside which a cart track leads SSW, marked by a waymark on an ash tree. The track skirts a wood, and then enters it to climb steeply through the woods and a meadow to approach the Hôtel Concorde at St Nizier-du-Moucherotte.

St Nizier, 1,100m (3,608ft), has a number of good hotels and *auberges*. The Hôtel du Bel Ombrage has a pleasant atmosphere and is reasonably priced; and there are more sophisticated hotels in the village if you wish. The village has an eleventh century parish church, much restored and with interesting modern glass and sculptures of the Virgin and of St Thérèse contrasting with an ancient font.

From the church it is possible to continue the walk to the summit of Le Moucherotte (*see* Walk 3A) and in any event it is worth taking the short detour to the viewpoint near the church. Otherwise, retrace your steps past the Hotel Concorde and down the D106 towards Grenoble, passing the road on the left signposted towards La Chaussère, to the point where the main road turns sharp left at 1,092m (3,583ft). A minor road leads straight ahead; to the right can be seen the Olympic ski jump. Take the path leading down half left at the point where the minor road joins the D106; the path is marked by red and blue markings on the top of a post and signposted to the Balcon Est and Le Moucherotte par Le Pas Est. (One of the great long walks of the area leads from here along the ridge of the Vercors to the Col de l'Arc and the Mont Aiguille.)

The path follows steeply down into mature, broad-leaved woodlands. At the first crossing take the upper path leading down east. The track here is rough and marked initially with bright red arrows. At the next fork in the

Les Trois Pucelles and Le Moucherotte

track bear right and continue downhill to reach a metalled track by a reservoir marked '*St Nizier Service des Eaux*' about half an hour after leaving the village. (In the Alps the *réservoirs* marked on maps are not vast expanses of water but are more generally concrete collection points for a *source captée*.)

Turn right and continue ESE along the metalled track towards the farm of Les Arcelles. At the point where four tracks meet turn sharp left downhill away from the farm; and walk northwards on a very small track towards a chalet. At the gate of the chalet turn sharp right on a larger path leading to the east – this is the old road from St Nizier. Follow this beneath the electricity powerlines, through the woods and down the crest of a long ridge until you emerge from the woods with a steep meadow on your right. Follow the track round a large bend until you see below you the old railway station which you passed on your ascent and from here retrace your steps to the Tour Sans Venin.

Walk 3A

It is possible to extend this walk by taking in the summit of Le Moucherotte 1,875m, (6,151ft). This adds some 3 hours to the total time of the walk, and a further 705m (2,312ft) of climb. The view from the summit of Le Moucherotte, both over Grenoble and the Massif de Belledonne, and over the valley of Lans-en-Vercors towards Charande, is well worth the effort.

Take the small road leading east from the north wall of the churchyard as far as the *Table d'Orientation* at 1,170m (3,744ft). Just before this, and immediately after a modern chalet, an earthen path leads uphill to the south. Follow this, past a reservoir, until it becomes metalled; and continue uphill in a generally southerly direction until the metalled road comes to an end by the entrance to a ski jump. From here a path is signposted to Le Moucherotte by La Cheminée. The path leads through small trees, out on to a meadow, and re-enters the woods not far before the line of the old cablecar to the summit of Le Moucherotte, now unused, and with its wire ropes rusting on the ground.

Pass over the fallen wires, and continue on the path around the contours of the hill until it turns abruptly uphill at the southern end of a clearing. The path follows the northern margin of the trees, and heads steeply uphill NE on hairpins to recross the line of the cablecar and become a well-made track heading eastwards through the trees. Paths lead off from this track to Les Trois Pucelles. Just before the track turns abruptly SW on the brow of a hill, a footpath, marked by a red and white waymark, leads uphill SW into the trees to the right of the path. Follow this towards La Cheminée, making sure to keep to the waymarked path; the path drops slightly under the line of the cablecar before making a long slow ascent through meadows and little trees around the western side of Le Moucherotte. After some 1.25km the path hairpins uphill, to approach the ruined huts which serviced the cablecar in its heyday. From here the path winds around to the E, to pass a deserted hotel and climb to a *Table d'Orientation* at the summit of the mountain.

To descend, take the track leading steeply downhill NNW just past the ruined huts. This curves around to the NE to pass under massive cliffs and descends rapidly through a gloomy combe to join the track from which the footpath to La Cheminée ascends.

Walk 4   Bois de Claret

Map no	IGN 3235 ouest
Distance	7.5km (4.7 miles)
Ascent	Negligible
Walking time	2 hours 45 minutes
Grading	Easy (1)

This is an easy walk through mature forests, giving views of the mountains surrounding the Vercors. The gradients are moderate and the path undulates, involving little change of height.

Take the D106C from Méaudre towards Les Griats, and the minor road leading north towards Les Colombets. It is possible to park at the corner where the path into the wood leads northwards at 1,044m (3,425ft).

The Walk

Take the right-hand path leading straight up the hill through a meadow towards the corner of the wood; the path to the left is marked 'Chemin Privé' (private road). As you climb through the meadow glance back towards the typical Alpine settlement of Les Griats and east to the Forêt de Guiney.

Enter the Bois de Claret by Le Grand Molard 1,136m, (3,727ft) and take the path leading NNE (another path leads off to the NW). The path is clearly waymarked with the Gentian mark of the Parc National du Vercors – in which it is path 26 – and with the black and yellow parallel bars of a local footpath. It leads north through the woods, undulating over the ridge and taking in summits at 1,150m and 1,139m (3,772ft and 3,736ft). Paths lead off to the NW at intervals; keep to the waymarked track because it is easy to get lost in the wood – twice on our walk we met the same jogger running from Méaudre to Autrans; on both occasions he was running in precisely the opposite direction to that which he supposed.

The views to the right through the trees are not spectacular; but they give an excellent impression of the ecology of the Alps: the valley floor given over to pasturage and to outdoor pursuits (note the outdoor centre (Centre de Plein

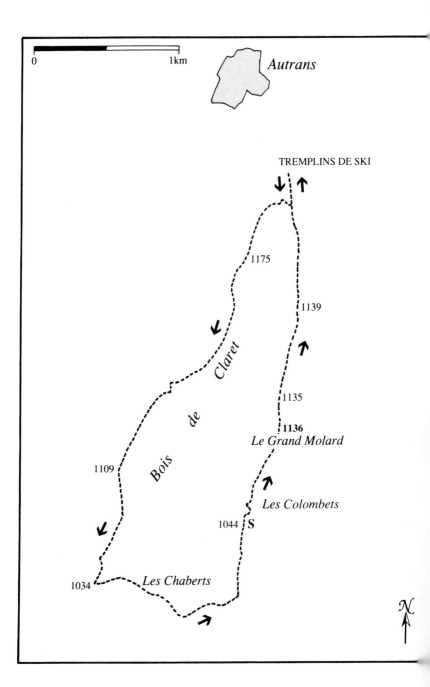

Autrans

TREMPLINS DE SKI

1175

1139

Claret

1135

1136
Le Grand Molard

de

1109

Bois

Les Colombets

1044 S

1034 Les Chaberts

N

Air) and caravan park at La Perrinière; the heavily wooded hills . The Bois de Claret has typical woodland vegetation and butterflies are common; occasionally in the sandy soil you can see the galleries of moles; and we were rewarded with the sight of a young mole nosing at the entrance to a gallery before scurrying to another tunnel.

Towards the northern end of the wood the path splits into three: the middle path is signposted to the *Tremplins de Ski* (Olympic Ski Jumps). Take this, uphill, until you reach the top of a ski-lift: the ski jump is just below. From here there is a rewarding view northwards to the village of Autrans, with Le Truc and Le Bouchet (Walk 5) to the NW and Charande (Walk 6) beyond.

Retrace your steps from the ski-lift to the point where the path split into three (at the point signposted to the *Tremplins de Ski*) and turn right (westwards). There is a black and yellow waymark (for a local path) and a gentian sign numbered 25 (Gentian Waymark 25) on a tree to the right. Follow path 25 south through the trees, avoiding the track on your right, until you reach a parcel of forest which was (in 1989) being well worked; sweet smelling pine logs lie alongside the track. Keep to the ridge, ignoring the track which leads steeply down to the right, and climb the track ahead marked by a yellow and black waymark. This track is used by forest vehicles and could be muddy in wet weather. Follow this up and round, taking care to follow the waymarks, until the path veers to the right by long balks of timber held in place by upright poles hammered into the ground. The path descends steeply westwards from this point and swings round to the south. In due course becomes a bridleway marked by an orange disc marked 'Vercors Equestre' as well as by Gentian Waymark 25. Follow the waymarks down between steep banks to leave the wood above the hamlet of Les Chaberts.

The path leads downhill through a meadow to the corner of a metalled road leading south and east at 1,034m (3,392ft). It is possible to continue southwards along path 25 to a summit at 1,071m (3,514ft) marked by the Croix des Albans and so to Méaudre (the track, well marked, leads off to the right of the metalled road as you reach the houses). Alternatively, turn left along the metalled road and follow it down past the Holiday Centre (sensitive modern architecture with an Alpine idiom) to the D106c at Piaillon. Follow the main road a short distance to the minor road leading up to Les Colombets and back to the start of the walk.

Walk 5   Bellecombe

Map no	IGN 3235 Ouest
Distance	7km (4.4 miles)
Ascent	390m (1,280ft)
Walking time	3 hours
Grading	Moderate (3)

From D106c on the road from Lans-en-Vercors to Autrans, turn right on to a minor road signposted to Le Bouchet and park the car at the junction of tracks at 1,118m (3,697ft).

The Walk

The path starts opposite a house and a barn with a red roof; a concrete signpost directs you to the Pas de Bellecombe. A pleasant white track leads up towards the woods and the steep gully which you will ascend. There are blue gentian waymarks; the view back towards the village is of a typically pastoral Alpine landscape.

When you reach the fork in the track at the edge of the wood take the right-hand path heading uphill; a blue Gentian Waymark 24 is on a tree to the left. The path climbs steeply uphill through mixed broad-leafed and coniferous woodlands and past some ugly concrete reservoirs. Follow the main track – a stony cart-track – up the hill, ignoring the small paths which lead off to the right. The path swings left and ascends, bearing 60° through tall fir trees; there is a wealth of meadow flowers, foxgloves and *clochettes* and, in season, wild strawberries. Beyond a stream – dry in summer – the path becomes rocky and climbs steeply uphill on hairpins, leaving the woods to meet a steep meadow from which there is a superb view down the valley and across the plateau of Autrans. At the top of the meadow, and after a climb of some 50 minutes, the path reaches a forest road at 1,500m (4,921ft).

Turn left along the forest road to approach a pylon. The road, which leads through mature forest, has very little traffic, although you may meet the odd forest vehicle trailing logs, or a mountain bike or two. Continue past the

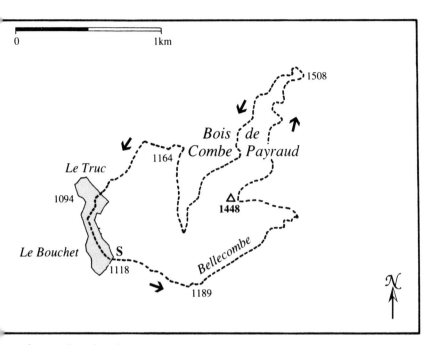

pylon at a large bend in the road, and after a walk along the contours of about 1.5km and a further five bends the road reaches a sharp hairpin bend at 1,508m (4,948ft). A signpost pointing uphill marks a number of paths; and from this point Walk 6 to the Pas de L'Ours and Charande begins. A little further along the road, on the left-hand side, is a signpost marking a path downhill to 'Autrans par le Guinchet'. The path is numbered 23 on a stone on the ground; it has the sign for the *Vercors Equestre*, although it is narrower than you would expect for a bridleway in Britain.

After an initial steep descent from the road, the path has a pleasant downhill gradient trending generally SW and, unlike some paths through woods in the region, is very easy to follow. The flowers are not, however, as prolific as on the ascent. A Gentian Waymark 23 greets you at intervals and, from time to time, there are views through the trees to the valley floor and the village of Autrans, to the left of which is the Bois de Claret and the Olympic ski jump of Walk 4. The wood is a mixture of beech, fir and pine; and there is a beautiful short passage over a gorge – le Ravin de Château Ver – with steep cliffs to left and right. Beyond, the path crosses a section of scree with a wealth of Alpine plants – harebells, marguerite, saxifrage – it is very well made and poses no difficulties. Thereafter it descends more steeply still through birch and hazel to a steep hairpin to the right. Follow the path round

The path from Le Bouchet to Bellecombe

the hairpin NNW, ignoring the small path leading ahead and uphill; just past the hairpin is a black arrow painted on a tree.

The path continues northwards downhill, approaching the foot of Le Ravin de Château Ver; at which it turns abruptly left and at 1,164m (3,819ft) descends steeply through flower studded meadows WNW towards a little road leading from Le Guinchet to Le Truc. When you reach the road turn left following the red arrow towards Le Truc (a sign on a tree marks the path you have descended – '*le Pas de l'Ours par le Guinchet 1h 30m No 23* '). Up on the left can be seen the pylon at the top of the walk, with Bellecombe beneath it.

Le Truc and Le Bouchet are attractive little hamlets; their traditional houses and farms are in marked contrast to the modern chalets of Autrans. The overhanging eaves, steeply pitched roofs and angled crow steps are designed for the snow, as are the woodpiles beside the houses. A typical fountain and horse trough is by the little square of Le Truc; over the barn door of the farm on the right are nailed a large number of tokens marking wins in the local cattle breeding competitions (_concours d'élevage_). Take the left-hand fork towards Le Bouchet, noting a little way along the road the blacksmith's forge with its harness for shoeing horses, and the picturesque woodmill and barn of La Fournelle, just before you return to the start of the walk.

Walk 6   Charande by the Pas de L'Ours

Map no	IGN 3235 ouest
Distance	6km (3.7 miles)
Ascent	201m (659ft)
Walking time	2 hours
Grading	Easy (2)

This walk offers some excellent ridge walking and rewarding views to the Massif de la Chartreuse and over fine meadows to Le Moucherotte and the Pic St Michel. It is, for all that, very easy. It is possible to combine it with Walk 5 to produce an extended and more stretching walk.

Take the forestry road which turns eastwards off the D106 just north of the *auberge* at the Col de la Croix Perrin and drive east past the Fontaine des Marcettes to the Bellecombe (Walk 5) and a pylon on the left-hand side of the road. Continue round a further four bends to the steep hairpin at 1,508m (4,948ft). Paths lead off to the east marked by the gentian waymark of the Vercors: take path 23 towards the Pas de l'Ours.

The Walk

The path is marked by blue and black waymarks and leads moderately steeply uphill; after about 150m it turns sharp right and heads south, clearly marked by an arrow on a tree and the Gentian Waymark 23. It levels out, and then goes slightly downhill to a meeting of tracks by a stream at 1,590m (5,217ft).

From here the path to the Pas de l'Ours leads back to the left, diagonally NE up the hill through a pine forest; it is marked by blue and black waymarks, and Gentian Waymarks 23 and 9. It approaches a small clearing just below the pass bright with unharvested yellow gentians (most of the gentians in the region are gathered to make Suze, a bitter apéritif). From the clearing it is a moderately steep climb to the pass at 1,649m (5,410ft) which is marked by a blue signpost and a Gentian Waymark 17.

Take the path signposted towards Charande which leads northwards to the left from the Pas de l'Ours. This forms a very easy ridge walk along the

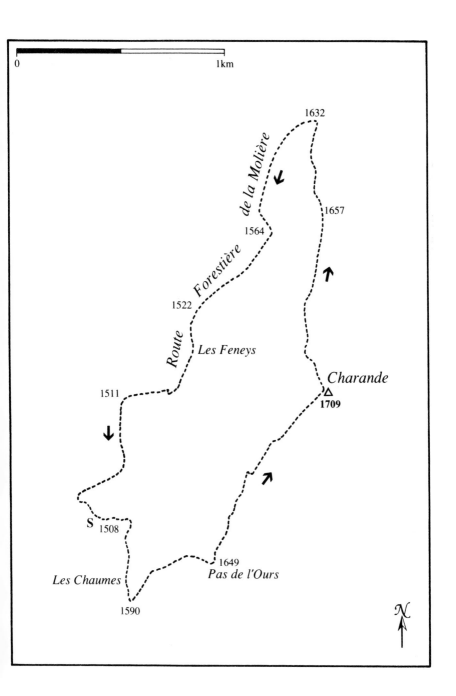

0   1km

1632

de la Molière

1657

1564

Forestière

1522

Route

Les Feneys

1511

Charande
1709

S 1508

1649
Pas de l'Ours

Les Chaumes

1590

N

edge of cliffs, below which is rich pasturage with scattered trees. Beyond, to the ESE are the Trois Pucelles and Le Moucherotte. The ridge is rich with a profusion of wild flowers – buttercups, gentian, harebells and rosebay willowherb, among others – and the air is scented with wild carnations. To the SE are the steep cliffs of the Gorges du Furon, giving visual proof of the assertion that as much of the Vercors is below ground level as above.

Follow along the edge of the cliffs (taking the right-hand fork where the path splits) towards Charande 1,709m (5,607ft). To the north is a panorama of the Massif de Chartreuse, with La Pinéa, Charmant Som and the Grand Som easily identifiable; and, to the right, Chamechaude and La Dent de Crolles. From the summit continue north along the ridge to La Molière. A notice on a tree indicates a hunting reserve (ACCA *Engins – Chasse Gardée*). Beyond, at the Pas du Tracollet 1,648m (6,391ft), the path splits into three. The left path is a short cut back to the forest road, and the right path leads on to the pasturage of La Molière – now a favourite place for children's summer camps. Continue on the centre path along the ridge past a white stone with red markings and the number 94, marking a forest boundary.

The track along the ridge continues down towards a saddle at 1,632m (5,354ft) where there is a picnic place and a car park. From here, follow the metalled forestry road downhill to the SW; on public holidays it may be busy, but there is pleasant walking on a track through the trees to the left of the road. At the steep hairpin at the Abri Forestier des Feneys 1,522m (4,993ft) take the forestry road continuing south into the Forêt de Bellecombe for 1.5km to regain the start of the walk. It is possible to buy drinks, omelettes, sandwiches and snacks in the Abri; the walk from there to the start of the walk follows easily along the contours and gives fine views through the trees towards Autrans.

Walk 6A

It is possible to combine Walks 5 and 6 to give a longer half day's walking. Take Walk 5 to the point where the path through the Bellecombe reaches the forest road to the east of the pylon. About 50m along the road towards the pylon a path leads SE uphill through long grasses and scattered trees to the Pas de Bellecombe 1,636m (5,367ft) on the ridge leading towards the Pas de l'Ours and Charande: the start of the path is indistinct. From the Pas de Bellecombe follow the ridge to rejoin Walk 6 at the Pas de l'Ours. Rejoin Walk 5 at the point on the forest road where path 23 is signposted towards Autrans par Le Guinchet. The total length of this combined walk is 11.25km (7 miles), involving a climb of 591m (1,939ft) and some 4$^1/_2$ hours walking.

Walk 7   La Balme-de-Rencurel

Map no	IGN 3235 ouest
Distance	5.25km (3.75 miles)
Ascent	300m (984ft)
Walking time	$2^1/_2$ hours
Grading	Moderate (3)

This is a pleasant woodland walk leading to two virtually unspoilt villages; despite the thick trees there are some fine views, particularly at the top of the walk. Navigation in the woods requires a little care; while the path is waymarked throughout, it is easy to stray from it and at one point on the return journey the waymarks disappear.

Take the D106 from Méaudre towards La Balme-de-Rencurel via the Gorges de la Bourne – a spectacular canyon carved out by the River Bourne. (If you have time, it is worth visiting the hydro-electric scheme in a massive cave on the opposite bank of the river.)

The Walk

The walk starts in the village square of La Balme-de-Rencurel on a little road leading NW between attractive old houses opposite a Bar Tabac and hotel: the house on the left with varnished shutters was formerly the Hôtel Rousset. After 150m cross a little bridge and climb left uphill past a rendered house with its woodpiles ready for winter. Take the second path on the right, marked by a signpost to Les Glénats and Les Antis, and follow this NE uphill through thick woods and around a hairpin. At the top of the hairpin is another signpost, nailed to a tree, to Les Glénats and Les Antis by local GR19.

The path, marked by yellow and red waymarks painted on stones, winds uphill through a deciduous wood. After a short but sharp climb it levels off by a dry stone wall and climbs northwards. Ignore the path heading left steeply uphill by a dry stone shelter built into the bank (you will come down this path on your return) and continue NNW on a clear path at the bottom of what looks like a cutting. At the end of the cutting – marked by a dry stone

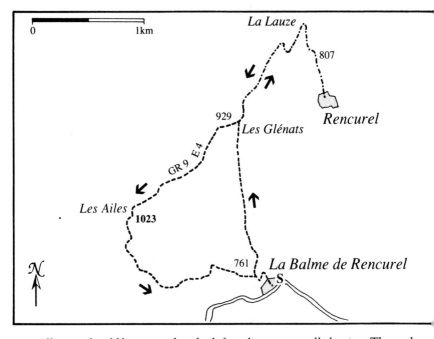

wall – you should bear round to the left and across a small clearing. The path then leads through a succession of clearings and meadows studded with wild roses and thorntrees, past a yellow waymark on a tree, and into a further wood, mainly of hazel, which is likely to be a good place for mushrooms in autumn.

The path emerges from the wood and climbs alongside another steep meadow; keep to the lower end of the meadow, passing woods to your left, until you see a solitary fir tree ahead. Pass to the left of this to join the GR9 at 929m (3,048ft), and turn right towards the hamlet of Les Glénats. There is a red and white GR marking on a rock to the left of the track. Beyond are more meadows set in a pastoral landscape not unlike Wales; it is difficult to realise that in Scotland this delicate landscape would qualify for Munro status!

The GR9 emerges by a television mast from which there is a wide view over the valley of Rencurel towards the cliffs of the Gros Martel 1,556m (5,105ft) and the Gorges de la Bourne. Turn left towards the village, past a house falling rapidly, and sadly, into ruin. The villagers call this *la maison de la grand -mère* (grandmother's house) after the last inhabitant. She had a family of eight children, and when she died they could not agree among themselves who should inherit. So the door hangs crazy on broken hinges, the roof is falling

House lintel, Les Glénats

in, rosebay willowherb grows in the cold grate, and jackdaws nest in the chimney.

The houses have carved mantels; the farm on the right, where one can buy cheese, has a cross and two fleurs-de-lys, with the date 1807, rudely carved but no doubt effective in keeping out the evil eye. The house on the left beyond the junction of the track and the minor road at 928m (3,045ft) has another carved mantel dated 1704, its design signifying – we were told – that man passes but the earth remains. The names carved into the mantel are those of the builder of the house and of its first owners. Behind the house is a lean-to, also belonging to the family of the grandmother, and also falling into ruin.

To continue into Rencurel see the description of Walk 8A below. Otherwise, retrace your steps south towards the television mast and along the GR9 to the point where you joined it. Continue SSW, climbing up through the wood and keeping to the waymarked path; do not miss the turn to the right where the path begins to ascend more steeply. The path is well made, with small rocks hammered into the ground in steep places; decayed dry stone walls in the woods suggest that the land was formerly more intensively used than today. At some 900m from the TV mast it joins the minor road from Le Violon. Turn left, and walk towards the hamlet of Les Ailes, at 1,023m (3,356ft) the highest point of the walk.

La Balme-de-Rencurel

The houses of Les Ailes are of unrendered stones and have a picturesque although somewhat bleak appearance. Just past the first house on the left is a waymark, and there is a signpost on the side of a further building to la Balme-de-Rencurel, with a Gentian Waymark 19, indicating a path between the houses. Follow this as it turns right and heads downhill SE, passing a meadow on the left and entering a wood. At a further narrow meadow you meet a path heading right and left; the right-hand path is signposted to Les Antis and La Goulandière. Turn left, noting the gentian sign, along a well-made path heading downhill; below, through the trees, you can see meadows. Follow the

Gentian Waymarks downhill, keeping to path 19 and ignoring the path to your right numbered 20. The path works its way downhill through thick underwood, clearly signposted to begin with, but then becoming less distinct and unmarked. Follow downhill to meet a broken dry stone wall; follow this eastwards towards a meadow, where the wall disappears, and then into a wooded combe past a forest marking numbered 44.

The path swings round to the north, heading steeply downhill until, after some 200m, it meets a path leading down to the right between banks with a Gentian Waymark 19 sign on a birch tree to the left. Follow this path eastwards down steep hairpins beneath beech trees – there is a thick beech mash underfoot – to meet the path by which you climbed to Les Glénats at the point where it entered the cutting by the dry stone shelter built into the bank. From here, it is a simple matter to retrace your steps to La Balme-de-Rencurel.

Walk 8 Environs of Rencurel

Map no	IGN 3235 ouest
Distance	4.5km (3 miles)
Ascent	280m (919ft)
Walking time	$1^1/_2$ hours
Grading	Easy (1)

This is an easy walk through picturesque open countryside; it offers the opportunity to visit a traditional blacksmith and can be combined with Walk 7 by those who want a more stretching experience.

The first part of the walk is on the route of GR9. It begins near the Nouvel Hôtel in the village of Rencurel approached via the D35 from La Balme-de-Rencurel.

The Walk

Walk up towards the church on the road leading left beyond the fountain. The church is not really worth a visit; but take the minor road signposted towards Le Pinet and Bellevue and leading NNE past the cemetery – drop in if you want to study the ebullience of French funeral art. From here, the road climbs gently beside meadows beyond which, to the east, are the Rochers de Gonson – a long line of limestone cliffs leading north from the flanks of the Gros Martel. To the west, across the valley, are the heavily wooded slopes of the Forêt Domaniale des Coulmes.

Pass the farm of Bellevue and a telephone relay station at the left-hand side of the road to reach the farm of Le Pinet. The farm has an attractive farmyard with a fountain; the path crosses diagonally across the yard (there is a red and white waymark) and passes to the right of a barn and through a gate to follow a cart-track leading north uphill between walnut trees. In the fields to the right of the path is another walnut orchard. Walnuts are an important local crop, and also the basis of the splendid local walnut wine.

Take the left-hand fork where the track divides and follow it round the side of the hill and into a wood through steep banks. The path comes out into a

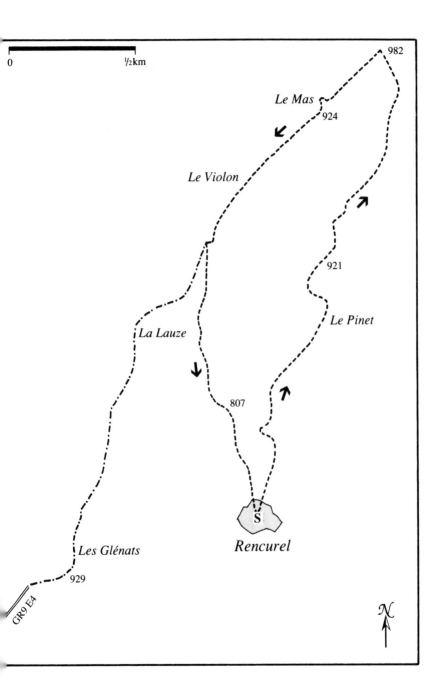

0   ½km

982

Le Mas
924

Le Violon

921

La Lauze

Le Pinet

807

Les Glénats
929

Rencurel
S

GR9 E4

N

meadow, then skirts the side of the wood and re-enters a wood of fir trees, finally emerging into meadows, some of them overgrown, and passing a ruined cottage on the right. From here a track leads eastwards to the Pas de la Chèvre. Continue north across a stream and past a renovated house. Leave the GR9 at the junction of the tracks at 982m (3,222ft) just before a ruined house, and turn left along a track marked with Gentian Waymark 15 leading SW through meadows and alongside a wood.

The track leads towards the Forges du Mas, where the blacksmith's art is still practiced by M Gerald Barier: his showroom is open from 10am to midday, and from 3pm until 7pm, apart from Sundays and holidays (tel 76 38 97 98). From here, follow the metalled track downhill; half left above you, you can see the television tower and the hamlet of Les Glénats (Walk 7); the hills to the right are heavily wooded with the Forêt Domaniale des Coulmes; and ahead is the Gros Martel.

Pass the farm of Le Violon on your left, loud not with stringed instruments but with the joyous barking of dogs and the mournful notes of the cowbells; a Gentian Waymark 15 on a telegraph pole to the right marks the route. The remains of a sundial is on the western wall of the farm. When you reach the metalled road D35 turn left to cross the bridge over the Doulouche and take the little road leading downstream south towards La Lauze – named after the flat rocks in the area. Continue in front of a range of buildings to cross a further bridge over the Doulouche and join a metalled road into the village, reaching the Nouvel Hôtel for a welcome drink at the end of your walk.

Walk 8A

It is possible to combine Walks 7 and 8 to produce a walk of some 12km taking 4 hours. From the hamlet of Les Glénats (Walk 7), just before the house with the carved mantel dated 1704 and in front of another house on the right, a green road leads downhill NNE below the line of the road to Le Violon. The green road is beautifully graded into the hillside and has dry stone revêtements and pavings, and gives views over meadows and copses to the village of Rencurel, clustered around its church: surely one of the most beautiful stretches of path in the Dauphiné. The track leads across a meadow towards a wood: at its entrance is a red and white GR waymark. The track leads into a wooded combe and hairpins back into meadows above Rencurel leading towards a house with a rusty corrugated iron roof. Turn right to pass in front of this house and to join Walk 8 just below the bridge over the Doulouche.

Walk down to the Nouvel Hôtel and follow the route of Walk 8 until you reach the bridge over the Doulouche by the farm of Le Violon. Cross the

Le Pinet, near Rencurel

bridge and, instead of taking the little road downhill to La Lauze, follow the metalled road uphill signposted to Les Glénats. This offers a relaxing walk, mostly along the contours, to the hamlet where the route of Walk 7 is reached.

Walk 9   Chauplane and the Rocher du Baconnet

Map no	IGN 3236 est
Distance	7km (4.3 miles)
Ascent	548m (1,798ft)
Walking time	$2^1/_2$ hours
Grading	Moderate (3)

This is a moderately difficult walk involving climbs over steeply inclined meadows and a descent along a ridge above steep cliffs; there are impressive views over the Lac de Monteynard and the Mont Aiguille.

Take the minor road from St-Michel-les-Portes to La Bâtie through spectacular gorges and cliffs – a country much more rugged than the northern Vercors. Mont Aiguille heaves itself up into the skies to the south, its immense limestone cliffs looking utterly unscalable. Here it was, however, that the art of mountaineering was first practised in the Alps in the early fifteenth century. At La Bâtie is a thatched cottage, unusual for the region. From the village drive towards the Col de l'Allimas and, before the col, take the unmetalled track to Chauplane. Park in the large gravel area about 100m down the track.

The Walk

Walk towards the picturesque hamlet of Chauplane. Here there are a number of carefully renovated houses: but for the universal desire for holiday homes Chauplane could have died. Pass a GR sign on your right to reach a barn with a new roof of corrugated iron. Beyond the barn at the bottom end of the hamlet turn uphill north and follow a path leading back past houses and a barn. Beyond is a grassy track bounded by a tumbledown dry stone wall. Pass through a fence, and head northwards across a meadow; the path here is ill-defined but leads uphill broadly NE parallel to the line of cliffs over to the left.

The meadow is rich with flowers – gentians, white Alpine thistles, clovers, wild carnations, autumn crocuses – and is haunted by butterflies and a profusion of crickets and grasshoppers (the grasshoppers are green; and the

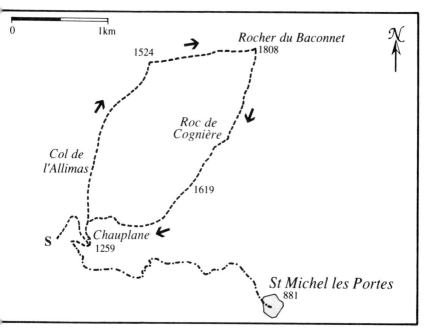

crickets are beige with red underbellies). Behind you as you climb are superb views of the Mont Aiguille, surrounded by thick woods and flanked by steep cliffs. Beyond is a wood of stunted trees, fir and ash; find your own path through its lower edge, past large heaps of stones, and work towards a gully to your left.

Leave the wood, still bearing NE, and head towards a col; pass through the curious iron cattle gate (in effect, a long tunnel through which the cattle must pass like players entering a football pitch) and make your way down to the cross on a knoll before you at 1,524m (5,000ft). From here there are fine views of the woods and pastures of the valley of Gresse-en-Vercors and the ski resort of La Ville, overshadowed by the bare cliffs of La Roche Rousse 2,105m (6,906ft) and the Rocher de Seguret. To the SW is Le Grand Veymont 2,341m (7,680ft), the highest mountain in the area.

Leave the cross to climb a short distance east, and then work your way north along the hillside, following sheep tracks across a combe. As you reach a further combe, turn east to climb the 283m (928ft) to the Rocher du Baconnet. While from time to time you can make use of sheep tracks, you will probably find it easier to make your own hairpins as you climb. Bilberries grow in profusion with sweet smelling wild carnations. The view west is fine; the slope falls away vertiginously to a flat valley bottom with mixed pasture and

Le Mont Aiguille

woods; the resort of La Ville (an eyesore needing a veil of snow); and above it the bare rock.

But the view eastwards from the summit is finer still. The mountainside falls away in sheer cliffs; to the ENE is the town of Monestier de Clermond, and beyond it the Lac de Monteynard, a vast expanse of water created by *Electricité de France* by damming the head waters of the Drac. To the SE are immense cliffs uplifted at the same angle as the meadow up which you have climbed; and the whole landscape is dominated by the Mont Aiguille.

From the summit it is an easy walk a few metres back from the cliff edge towards Chauplane. From time to time the cliff is broken by gullies; the *gouffre* below the Roc de Cognière is particularly fine and here you may see a hawk wheeling effortlessly on the wind. As you descend the grass becomes smoother; the path leads through trees along the side of the scarp, and then joins the meadow through which you made your ascent.

Walk 9A Le Chemin du Facteur

If you can arrange suitable transport the walk may be extended from Chauplane to St-Michel-les-Portes by way of the Chemin du Facteur. A local GR marked by a yellow and red waymark leads downhill eastwards from

Chardon des Alpes

Chauplane just before the barn and renovated house, and immediately to the left of a house which, in 1989, was in course of renovation. The path passes a spring to reach a T-junction marked by a signpost indicating *le Chemin du Facteur, Numéro 5*.

Turn left, and head downhill on a path marked by the Gentian Waymark 5. The path descends SE through pine woods, through which can be seen from time to time the peak of the Mont Aiguille, and, to the left above you, the dramatic cliffs of the Rochers des Côtes. Follow the path gently downhill until you reach a junction. Take the upper path leading slightly uphill; if you miss it, you will reach a blue cross painted on a rock in the pathway, with an arrow pointing back; beyond the cross the lower path becomes impassable at a landslip. The upper path leads uphill on six steep hairpins across scree to enter a birchwood. Here it almost disappears; be careful not to miss the point where it turns back on itself and hairpins down the hillside.

In places the path is quite overgrown; it descends on hairpins, trending eastwards, and at one point leads beside a steep gorge and over scree. In due course it reaches some slightly scrubby meadows and becomes more distinct, although still somewhat overgrown. Follow down past a cattle trough; the village becomes visible below you to the right; and you will see quarry workings on the opposite hillside. From here the path falls steeply to the right between overgrown banks to meet a cart-track which leads into the village of St-Michel-les-Portes.

Walk 10   La Roche and the Table D'Orientation

Map no	IGN 3236 est
Distance	4km (2.5 miles)
Ascent	92m (302ft)
Walking time	2$\frac{1}{2}$ hours
Grading	Easy (2)

This is an easy walk with no difficult gradients, for the most part on easily identified tracks. While the walk is at a relatively low level – the highest point is at 1,045m (3,428ft) – it offers fine views of the Southern Vercors; and the hamlet of La Roche, with its green roads, its fountain where nymphs bathe, its traditional haycocks, and its exquisite belvédère, is one of the most peaceful places in the region.

From N75 at Monestier-de-Clermont, take the minor road at the southern end of the station signposted to Col de Fraisse. Park at the Col 947m, (3,107ft); the Col is to the south of a hill surmounted by a telecommunications mast. A signpost on a tree points to the Col de Maissenas, the *Table d'Orientation*, La Roche and Le Puy.

The Walk

Take the road to Le Puy, which is marked by yellow and red waymarks; it leads gently downhill eastwards through woods. After a bend southwards, about 500m from the start of the walk, a track leads off to the right which is signposted to the Col de Maissenas. Follow this uphill until you reach a meadow and a meeting of tracks; a signpost on a tree indicates, to the right, the Col de Maissenas, '*Premier virage à gauche* ' (first left turn), and the *Table d'Orientation* to the left.

Continue along the track towards the *Table d'Orientation*; there are fine views northwards towards the television tower, and NW to the high mountains of the Trième. The track leads between two meadows; at the point where it re-enters the wood a path leads off to the right marked '*Table d'Orientation de Côte Rouge No 15* '. There is also an old signpost to the *Table d'Orientation* on

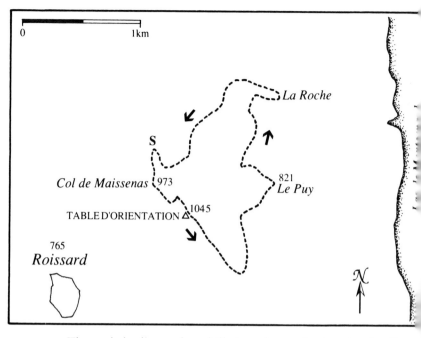

a tree. The path leads steeply uphill through woods, then levels off to approach the *Table d'Orientation*.

The *Table d'Orientation* was placed here by the Touring Club de France in 1912. An inscription states that the Côte Rouge is at longitude 3° 68' 80", latitude 49° 87' 50", and altitude 1,045m (3,428ft). Despite its relatively low altitude it offers magnificent views over the Lac de Monteynard and Mont Seneppi to the east; the northern Vercors and Le Moucherotte to the north; and the heights of Mont Aiguille and the Grand Veymont to the SW.

From the *Table d'Orientation* continue SSE on a narrow path through thick low trees; the aquamarine waters of the lake are visible to your left. After a steepish descent you come to a crossing of the tracks; the path ahead is virtually obliterated. Turn left here, and continue downhill (a Gentian Waymark 15 is on a tree) to meet an ancient cart-track heading steeply downhill northwards. At a crossroads continue north; through the trees, on the opposing hillside, can be seen the hamlet of La Roche.

The path swings NW and approaches Le Puy, which is approached down steps to the right-hand side of the track. The path leads along the SE side of the houses. From the houses take the forest road heading sharp left NE; do not take the path leading straight on to Herbelon. The track leads slightly uphill round the contours; it becomes grassy and slightly overgrown, as it passes

Lac du Monteynard from La Roche

through short Mediterranean pines, under telephone wires and through an electric fence – easily opened – before swinging east along a *balcon*.

The path bends towards a barn on the hillside; just below the bend is a fountain in which, as we walked, we disturbed a beautiful girl bathing. The hamlet consists of a barn and a cottage, now used as a holiday home; beyond it a short path leads eastwards to a belvedere giving a view over the lake.

The return from the belvédère gives fine views of Chauplane (Walk 9). From the hamlet a green track leads ENE; in late summer there are traditional haycocks in the fields to the right-hand side of the track; and the television tower above the start of the walk is visible to the west. The path has an easy gradient leading imperceptibly upwards; ignore the forestry track which leads down the hill, and continue past meadows and back into woods until the path becomes metalled and passes, on the left-hand side, the path which you took uphill to the *Table d'Orientation*.

Walk 11   L'Aiguille de Quaix

Map no	IGN 3234 est
Distance	4km (2$^1/_2$ miles)
Ascent	242m (794ft)
Walking time	2$^1/_2$ hours
Grading	Moderate (3); difficult passage to summit (6)

This is a pleasant short walk through woods to one of the spectacular limestone outcrops of the Chartreuse – the Aiguille (Needle) de Quaix 1,143m (3,750ft).

From D105 from St Egrève through Proveysieux to Pomaray; turn sharp right towards Planfay immediately after Hôtel de la Pinea; follow the road to a sharp left turn at 879m (2,883ft); park on a large gravel area on the left-hand side of the road beyond a farm.

The Walk

The path leads diagonally uphill to the SE from farm buildings on the eastern side of the road which leads north from a sharp bend beyond Planfay at 879m (2,883ft). It starts opposite a well-restored stone house with new shutters and dormer windows by the first barn on the right following the sharp bend; a sign indicates *Passage de Tracteurs*. It passes through an orchard, and skirts along the edge of the woods; steep meadows fall away to the right and there are views down towards Grenoble. L'Aiguille de Quaix can be seen jutting up half right; from this angle it looks unscalable. When you reach a crossing of tracks take the track leading eastwards, passing a hut on your left.

Ford the Ruisseau de Furetas and take the left-hand path leading uphill towards a pinewood. The track, which is sometimes muddy, winds clearly up through the trees along the hillside to approach another stream in the Bois Ronzier; here it turns sharp right southwards, fording the stream. Continue uphill, passing a red forestry mark on a tree on the right-hand side of the track. The path climbs round through beech trees, then heads steeply uphill past a red forestry notice. At the ridge you reach a gravel track heading NE and,

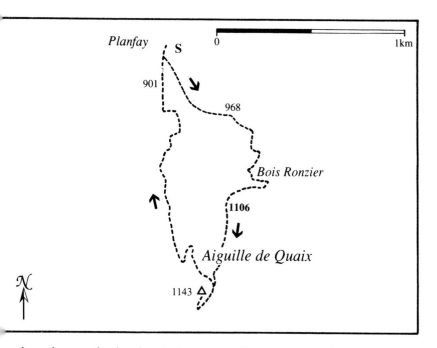

through steep banks, downhill to the SW; turn sharp right just before reaching this track and walk westwards along the ridge by way of an earthen path between mixed pine trees and beech. At a summit on the ridge are a number of forestry marks, including a boulder between two birch trees on the right, and yellow pin-men atop horizontal bars.

A wide, well-made path heads down the ridge SSW. The summit of l'Aiguille de Quaix is hidden by trees; far over to the east can be seen the eternal snows of Belledonne. The gradient is slight, and the path easily followed until it becomes indistinct on the final ascent to the summit. Climb up through the trees, bearing slightly left; there is something of a scramble as you reach the rock at the base of the summit. From here, if you scramble a short distance up the rocks, are views northwards towards la Pinéa and Chamechaude. Follow the path around the foot of the east face of the Aiguille, which rises steeply above you; and at the southern end of the cliffs climb up to a gully, or *brèche*, on the summit ridge. From here you can see the hamlets of the Le Gua and Planfay, and the house on the road at the start of the walk.

From this point it is possible to ascend to the summit by way of a steep scramble up the summit ridge; the views from the gully are, however, almost as good as those from the summit; and the scramble is not for those afflicted with vertigo!

Retrace your steps along the foot of the eastern face of the Aiguille. From here you can take the same route back to the start of the walk or, as an alternative, return by way of Michaletière to the west of the route upwards. A path takes off NW in the steep woods at the northern foot of the Aiguille, about 100m beyond a large fallen tree. It descends in steep hairpins to meet a well-made path following the contours of the hill. Turn left, southwards, along this path, and follow it until you cross a hump in the ground; to the right is a rock whose top is painted red. Head downhill towards a tree on which is painted a yellow cross; and beyond this turn right into a meadow.

Cross the meadow (it is necessary to climb through a barbed wire fence) to a point half-way along its northern edge by a ruined hut. Here a track leads northwards to Michaletière. A little way down the track is a spring under a beech tree. Further down the track fords the Ruisseau de Furetas by a large rock and turns sharp left to meet the metalled road from Pomaray. Turn right, and walk up the road to the starting point.

Despite their closeness to Grenoble the hamlets in this area are picturesque; there is little modern building and many of the houses have retained their rough stone walls without any rendering. The Hôtel de la Pinéa in Planfay has a delightful terrace and an area for playing *boules* and makes a pleasant place to finish your walk.

Walk 12   La Pinéa and Habert du Col de Porte

Map no	IGN 3234 est
Distance	10km (6.2 miles)
Ascent	621m (2,037ft)
Walking time	5$\frac{1}{2}$ hours
Grading	Moderate (3)

This walk offers a moderately stiff climb to one of the prettier peaks in the Chartreuse – La Pinéa 1,771m (5,810ft). There is some pleasant ridge walking and fine views from the summits. The walk can be extended by taking in the Balme de l'Air on the summit ridge towards Charmant Som.

Take the D512 from Grenoble to Le Sappey-en-Chartreuse; turn left at Col de Palaquit on to the D57 to Sarcenas; 0.5km beyond Sarcenas take the minor road signposted to Guilletière; turn right at Guilletière to Gervais. The walk starts from the farm of Gervais at the top of the metalled road from Guilletière and by a typical fountain.

The Walk

Take the left-hand track up the hill past a bright red fire hydrant numbered 13 and through a wood; as you enter the wood note the yellow and red waymark of a local GR on a tree and the yellow waymark opposite it. After 200m take the sharp bend to the left indicated by a yellow and red waymark; the path passes through a bank and turns right to follow the edge of the wood NNW. The path, which is ancient and well made, re-enters the wood at 1,217m (3,993ft) under immense birches. To the left from here can be seen the summit of La Pinéa at 1,771m (5,810ft).

The single red marks on the trees mark the limits of parcels of forest and should not be confused with waymarks. The path zigzags up through the woods to meet a forestry track; turn left and follow it to the next corner where you turn right on a track which heads northwards uphill. Follow the track uphill for 200m to where it forks; here turn right northwards: there is a waymark on a rock to your left. (Note the crossed waymark on the path

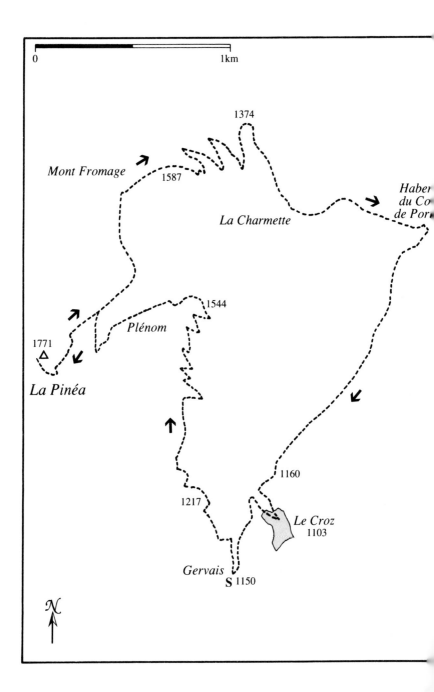

0   1km

Mont Fromage

1374

1587

La Charmette

Haber
du Co
de Por

1544

Plénom

1771

La Pinéa

1160

1217

Le Croz
1103

Gervais

S 1150

N

72

leading west, indicating that you should not go that way.) The path follows the contours, slightly downhill, to meet Le Pissou Torrent after some 30 minutes walking: there are fine views to the right towards Gervais, Sarcenas and the Massif de Belledonne beyond.

In summer Le Pissou is almost dry, and crossing it on rocks and balks of wood presents no difficulty. The path leads east up the opposite bank; over your left shoulder is the peak of La Pinea. At the top of the hill leading from the Torrent is a tree with a large red 'G' painted on it and a yellow and red waymark: turn left and continue uphill. To the SW you can see Le Moucherotte; and far below the city of Grenoble spread out in its valley.

The path climbs the hill on well-graded hairpins, flanked by harebells, wild strawberries and many other flowers; we met many butterflies and found some (now rare) Martagon lilies. Le Néron opens up to the SW. The path approaches the Torrent again, then turns away up further hairpins to meet a broad avenue at 1,544m (5,065ft) after a climb of 400m (1,312ft), about an hour's walk from the start. A signpost directs you left to La Pinéa and Charmant Som; to the right is Le Col de Porte.

Follow the yellow and red waymarks left to reach the Pré de Plénom; ignore the path to the right where the GR trends slightly downhill. Cross the prairie by its length; the path is well-defined in thick grasses. Behind you rises the massive bulk of Chamechaude. Re-enter the forest, taking care at the source of the Pissou Torrent where it is muddy underfoot. About 100m beyond the source there is a signpost; turn right here and ascend the hill northwards to the ridge. At the ridge there is a signpost to La Pinéa (to the left) and Charmant Som (to the right). A conveniently placed tree trunk provides a pleasant picnic spot.

Climb the path SW up the hill past a tree with a red mark and a large letter 'I'. The path follows round the SE side of the mountain; where there are a wealth of flowers to be found – *clochettes*, wild carnations, parchment coloured foxgloves, campanules. It is something of a scramble to reach the top, and there are steep drops below you. To the north you can see Charmant Som, with the village of St-Pierre-de-Chartreuse in the valley below it; to the east is Chamechaude and in the NE distance you can, on a clear day, make out Mont Blanc.

Retrace your steps to the fallen tree trunk where the path from Gervais reached the ridge, and continue along the ridge towards Charmant Som. Ignore the path to the right as you approach a tree with a large 'B' painted on one side and 'I' on the other, and continue on the waymarked path climbing steadily towards Montvernet 1,628m (5,341ft); in places, trees have fallen across the track. After Montvernet the path swings round through a beautiful

L'Aiguille de Quaix from the summit of La Pinéa

meadow with a wealth of wild flowers, and leaves the wood to reach a viewpoint marked by a notice board.

From this point it is an easy walk to Charmant Som along the ridge of La Balme de l'Air. If, however, you have insufficient time for this, retrace your steps into the wood to find a not very clearly defined path heading left downhill directly towards Chamechaude. (Just beyond this path, on its southern side, is a tree with a yellow and red waymark above which is a single red band.) The path broadens into a cart-track and becomes more clearly defined just beyond the trees; it descends the hill in hairpins trending generally NE. After skirting a meadow and passing through ancient pine trees it meets the end of a made-up gravel road heading ENE. Follow this left to meet a metalled road at the ski resort of the Habert du Col de Porte.

The Hôtel Rogier at the Habert has an agreeable bar and would make a pleasant stopping place. The cart-track to Gervais passes under powerlines at the point where the gravel road meets the metalled road; an electricity substation is on the right and there is a large 'J' painted on a tree at the start of the track. The path descends steeply, giving fine views of meadows to the left and occasionally falling between steep banks. After about 1.75km the track reaches a road end at the hamlet of Le Croz; cross the Pissou Torrent and take the track heading uphill on the right bank of the stream. Turn sharp left where the track is crossed by another, and head south away from the Pissou. The path follows the upper limit of the meadows towards Gervais and the start of the walk; from it are fine views of the wooded hills of the Chartreuse and, in the distance beyond, the jagged peaks of Belledonne.

Walk 13   Charmant Som

Map no	IGN 3234 est
Distance	3km (1.8 miles)
Ascent	190m (623ft)
Walking time	1¹/₂ hours
Grading	Easy (2); difficult alternative descent (5)

Charmant Som, as its name implies, is one of the prettiest of the Chartreuse range; and the walk to the summit 1,867m (6,125ft) from the Bergerie at the Chalets du Charmant Som, while steep, is little more than a stroll. But from the summit are magnificent views across the wooded valleys of the Chartreuse to Belledonne and the Vercors; and it is possible from here to form an overview of the Chartreuse range. In the ratio of rewards to effort, Charmant Som scores very high.

Take the D512 northwards from La Tronche to Col de Porte via Le-Sappey-en-Chartreuse. At Col de Porte bear left along the D57d to the Habert du Col de Porte – a small ski resort where, in winter, youngsters come to learn the elementary skills of the *art du ski*. The hotel here has a somewhat austere bar where it is possible to take a simple *plat du jour* or a beer. For a longer walk, start the walk here and take the metalled road uphill, and along hairpins the 5.25km (3.25 miles) to the Chalets du Charmant Som. The road from the Habert is, in any case, closed in winter; and it offers a delightful winter walk or cross country ski route.

The Chalets comprise an inn – the Auberge du Charmant Som – and a shepherd's bothy – the Bergerie.

The Walk

The path to the summit begins to the right of the chalets, and leads clearly across the close-cropped grasses to the shoulder of the lower summit SSW of the true summit. The meadows are rich grazing; and the minor key of the cowbells follows you up the hill. Take the path a few hundred metres NNW above the chalets to a junction in the paths; here take the path leading due

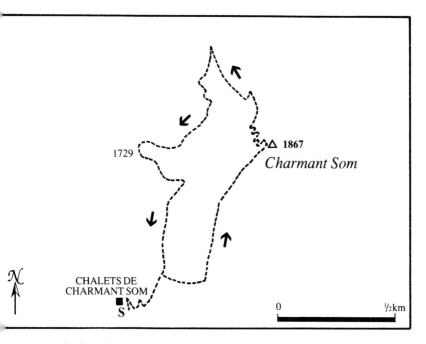

1729

△ 1867
Charmant Som

CHALETS DE
CHARMANT SOM

0   ½km

east towards the ridge leading up to the lower summit of the mountain, passing a deep gulf in the limestone to the right. The climb to the ridge is somewhat stiff, but is nevertheless very easy walking. From the ridge opens up a view of the valley of St-Pierre-de-Chartreuse and of Grand Som. Turn left and climb northwards towards the lower summit; the summit is rocky, but it is not necessary to scramble.

Follow the summit ridge across sometimes tricky boulders to the true summit of Charmant Som 1,867m (6,125ft). From the summit are views northwards to the Désert de la Grande Chartreuse and the monastery itself, nestling under the mass of the Grand Som (Walks 15 and 16); to the west are the massive limestone cliffs of Grande Sure beyond the Forêt de Génieux; southwards is the ridge of the Balme de l'Air leading to the pinnacle of La Pinéa(Walk 12), and eastwards the long wall of Belledonne, with the eternal snows gleaming in the sunlight.

From the summit you may retrace your steps to the Auberge du Charmant Som or take an alternative route leading northwards which is, however, of considerable difficulty. The route begins with a steep scramble down a chimney leading northwards from the summit of Charmant Som; it is marked by green and orange waymarks; and it is essential to keep to the waymarked path. At the foot of the chimney the path leads in a great hairpin across a steep grassy slope falling away to scree. Some 200m below the hairpin a path joins from the south. Follow this southwards through hairpins and alongside steep cliffs to a further meeting of paths at 1,729m (5,673ft). From here regain the Chalet du Charmant Som by way of the path leading to the left south-east beneath the cliffs, and then along a gentle slope across the meadow, rejoining the path by which you ascended 100m above the chalets.

The Auberge du Charmant Som offers a variety of drinks and food, including the local delicacy *fromage blanc.* Beyond it to the left is the shepherd's hut – well worth a visit to see the massive copper fermenting vessels and great cheeses ripening on tables in the gloom and on the windowsills and to buy *fromage blanc* from the magnificently bearded shepherd or his wife.

Walk 14   Col de la Charmette to Charmant Som by Le Pré Batard

Map no	IGN 3234 est
Distance	8km (5 miles)
Ascent	606m (1,988ft)
Walking time	$3^1/_2$ hours
Grading	Difficult (6)

This is a splendid, though demanding, walk to the summit of what is to many the prettiest mountain in the Chartreuse – hence its name of Charmant Som, the charming summit. As with Walk 13 there are fine views of the Chartreuse from the summit ridge; and this route is likely to be far less frequented than the easier routes to the summit.

Take the D105 northwards from St-Egrève to Col de la Charmette. (The road is closed beyond Pomaray from the first snowfall of winter.) In the middle of the road at the Col is a charming oratory with a statue of la Vièrge; there is ample parking space.

The Walk

Take the forest track heading slightly downhill NE signposted (on a tree on the right-hand side) to La Fontaine de l'Oursière and Chemin de la Cochette. After a short descent the track climbs NW along the side of the hill through trees through which, to the right, can be seen the cliffs of Charmant Som.

Take the right-hand path where the track forks and climb uphill east on a path between two cliffs; after a short stiff climb the path rejoins the track and continues more gently uphill towards the Fontaine de l'Oursière (the spring of the bear), which, despite its romantic name, has been piped into a large metal cattle trough. Beyond, the path veers to the left marked by orange arrows to climb steeply to the Pré Batard, which is reached about 30 minutes from the start of the walk.

The cliffs of Charmant Som climb steeply above you to the right of a gully; and the summit is hidden behind them to the SE. The path however turns

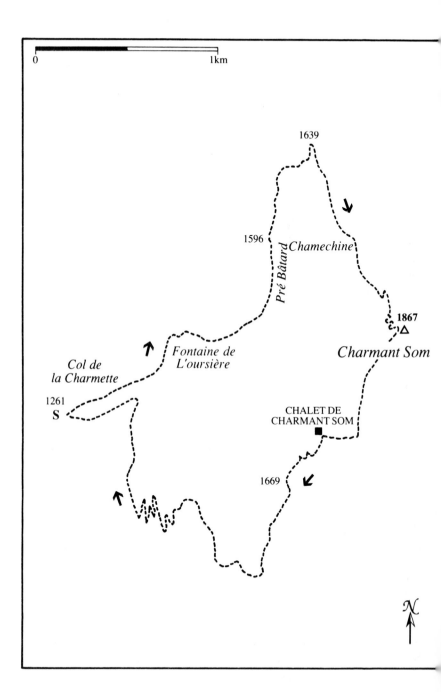

0   1km

1639

Chamechine

1596

Pré Bâtard

1867
△

Charmant Som

↑

*Fontaine de
L'oursière*

*Col de
la Charmette*

1261
S

CHALET DE
CHARMANT SOM
■

1669

↖

↗

N
↑

NNE and continues along the length of the pasture, marked by red arrows on the rocks. A profusion of gentians grows in the meadow; and wild thyme grows by the path. Pass a little circular mud splash at 1,590m (5,217ft) and approach a saddle beside which is another deep dew pond. From here the path climbs steeply to the right, indicated by orange arrows on the rocks, to reach a ridge from which is a fine view of La Correrie, La Grande Chartreuse and Grand Som, and, to the east, the Massif de Belledonne.

The path heads SSE a little way below the crest of the ridge, then climbs through a gully marked by orange arrows. Far down to the right can be seen the Col de la Charmette and the start of the walk. A certain amount of scrambling is necessary in the gully; but you are rewarded by the increasing richness and diversity of the flowers and by views of the summit of Charmant Som ahead. The path is clearly marked through the rocks; it makes a slight descent southerly through a meadow towards an orange and green arrow and then reaches a massive grassy slope which is crossed on an immense hairpin. The ground falls away very steeply to a scree slope, but the path itself is well-graded. Beyond, a green and orange marker points uphill into a chimney which requires a steepish, and rather difficult, scramble to the summit 1,867m (6,125ft). The route is clearly waymarked; and it is essential to keep to it.

From the summit are wide views across the Chartreuse and over to Belledonne in the east and the Vercors to the SW. Follow the summit ridge across sometimes tricky boulders to the lower summit of Charmant Som 1,729m (5,673ft). Below can be seen the Bergerie du Charmant Som and meadows rich with cattle.

Make your way down to the Bergerie on an easy path well-marked across cropped grass. The Auberge du Charmant Som and the Bergerie are well worth a visit – *see* Walk 13.

Take the little metalled road leading south downhill from the chalets, round a bend and over a bridge. As you turn the bend you can see La Pinéa (Walk 12) ahead of you. Take the forestry track leading westwards from the right-hand side of the metalled road some 600m from the chalets; follow this around the hillside NW, through meadows and into the woods where it curves round to the south.

Just before the last bend of the track a path leads steeply downhill to the right. At the start it is somewhat difficult to find because of forestry working; but it soon becomes clear; it descends on pleasantly graded hairpins through mixed woods, trending generally west. After seven hairpins and a long stretch NNW you find yourself walking parallel to a *chemin de tirage*, or forest track along which trees are dragged. (For those taking this walk in reverse, the path

Le Col de la Charmette

uphill is marked by a red arrow on a post by the side of the *chemin de tirage*.)

Turn right on to the forestry track, follow it north and, after a few hundred metres, west through tall pine trees to the Col de la Charmette and the start of the walk.

Walk 15　Environs of La Grande Chartreuse

Map nos	IGN 3234 est; 3333 ouest
Distance	$4^1/_2$km (2.8 miles)
Ascent	250m (820ft)
Walking time	$1^1/_2$ hours
Grading	Easy (1)

This is an easy walk in the immediate surroundings of La Grande Chartreuse, the monastery founded by St Bruno in the twelfth century. The *désert* (wilderness) of Chartreuse was chosen by St Bruno as the cradle of the Carthusian order because its difficult access guaranteed solitude and peace; indeed, the road from St-Laurent-du-Pont was not built until the nineteenth century. Even today the whole area has a palpable aura of tranquillity. The former guesthouse of the Monastery, La Correrie, is now a museum of Carthusian life and history; while you cannot visit the monastery itself, here you can see replicas of the cells and gardens occupied by the brothers and displays depicting the life and work of the order. *Correrie*, incidentally, means study; and in the library of Edinburgh University the areas set aside for private study are called carrells.

Travel to La Correrie on the D520b from St-Pierre-de-Chartreuse to St-Laurent-du-Pont.

The Walk

The walk starts at the entrance of the avenue leading to the monastery. The avenue is closed to motor traffic (there is ample parking at La Correrie) and is flanked by mature beeches and ash trees; white cliffs gleam to either side of the valley above steep meadows and woodlands.

After some 200m you enter the '*Zone de Silence du Désert de Chartreuse* '; take the right fork past the yellow and red GR waymark on a tree to the left and follow the metalled drive leading due north towards the monastery. Above on the right are the white cliffs of the Rocher de Combe Chaux. A cross is on the left-hand side, and a wall of immense boulders on the right.

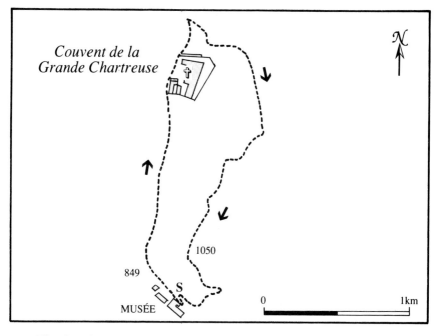

Couvent de la Grande Chartreuse

1050

849

S

MUSÉE

0   1km

The first buildings you come across are the stables of the monastery to the right: note the stables' round tower and wooden palings, and the spires of the gatehouse beyond; and to the left is the new guesthouse and a woodshed. Beyond the buildings, on the hill to the right, is a calvary; and where the driveway crosses an ancient bridge there is a signpost to Notre Dame de Casalibus and to the Grand Som – the track which starts Walk 16.

Take the track up the hill below the calvary towards the Grand Som. As you pass by the Chartreuse you may hear the bells tolling out the canonical hours and echoing from the rocks to the east. When you are level with the calvary you can see down into the monastery buildings – the cloisters and cells for the friars; the rank of buildings to house the members of the order worldwide; the great abbey church.

Follow the track to the gate at the edge of the wood, and take the track heading right into the wood. After a few metres there is a signpost to La Correrie; on the right is a notice warning that entrance to the forest is reserved for the members of the community – 'Accès réservé au monastère'. The track is heavily rutted and could be muddy in wet weather; it approaches close to the cliffs and begins to climb steeply. A track leads off to the left towards the summit of the Grand Som; there is a signpost to La Correrie pointing

85

Le Grand Som

southwards. A wealth of rockflowers cluster in the cliffs; and, in season, there
are wild raspberries just beyond the signpost.

The path is well made and nicely graded, although at one point you must
climb over a fallen tree. As you begin to descend there is a view over the gorge
of the Mort Rivau. You reach a great hairpin and continue downhill westerly,
crossing a bridge over a torrent made of vast treetrunks; when you reach the
next hairpin turn left and take the path down to the right leading along the
side of the wood: there is a yellow and red waymark on a rock to the left-hand
side of the path. About 100m below a little path leads off through the woods
down to the right: take this down to a signpost to the Grand Som at which
point turn right (if you begin to ascend again on the path after the signpost
you have gone too far). Below are the roofs of La Correrie. The track leads
down, past a notice marking the boundary of the *zone de silence*, and towards
the car park near the start of the walk.

Walk 16 Grand Som

Map nos	IGN 3234 est; 3333 ouest
Distance	14km (9 miles)
Ascent	1,147m (3,763ft)
Walking time	$6^{1}/_{2}$ hours
Grading	Difficult (6)

This is one of the most demanding walks in the Chartreuse, involving a lengthy climb to the summit of Grand Som, the Great Summit, 2,026m (6,647ft). It is definitely not for softies; but it is within the capability of moderately experienced walkers; and quite small children do attempt it.

Travel to La Correrie on the D520b from St-Pierre-de-Chartreuse to St-Laurent-du-Pont.

The Walk

The walk begins from La Correrie and takes the same route as Walk 15 to the wood-shed beyond the monastery; note the summit of the Grand Som to the NNE as you walk along the avenue to the monastery. Beyond the wood-shed is a signpost; ignore the path uphill to Grand Som and follow the sign on the left to Notre Dame de Casalibus 1.5km. The track passes a small reservoir which was formerly used to power the water mill of the Grande Chartreuse. Continue uphill, passing a path to the left signposted to Le Billon par Chemin du Pavé, and then a massive causeway of dressed stones to the right. Ahead and above you can be seen the Petit Som.

Beyond a hairpin at 1,140m (3,740ft) a red tiled building comes into view among the trees; this is the chapel of Casalibus. Unfortunately the chapel is kept locked, but through the windows can be made out a simple altar, walls painted to look like marble, wooden panels and two round arched windows. A little way through the woods to the NE is the chapel of St Bruno, beautifully perched on top of a rock above the clearing where the saint had the vision which led to the founding of his order. Below the chapel, to the left of the path, is a fountain marked with the letters FDSB (*Fide Diem St*

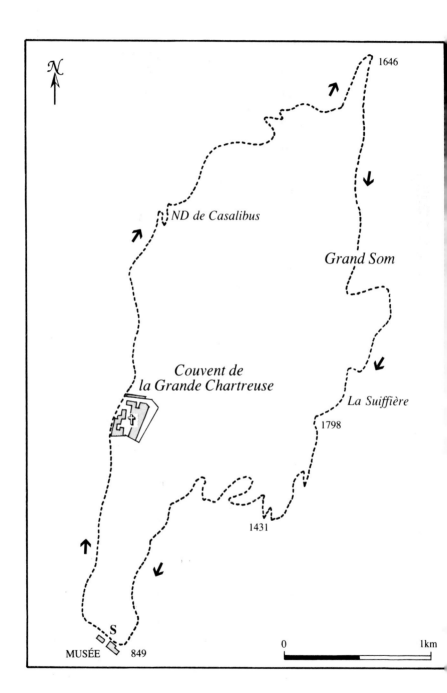

N

1646

ND de Casalibus

Grand Som

Couvent de
la Grande Chartreuse

La Suiffière

1798

1431

S

MUSÉE   849

0   1km

88

The Bergerie, Le Grand Som

Bruno); and above the door of the chapel a Latin inscription *Sacellum St Brunonis hic est locus in quo St Hugo Gratiano Politanis Episcopus vidit deum sibi dignum constituenten habitaculum.*

Retrace your steps to the chapel of Casalibus, and take the path leading uphill eastwards just to the south of the chapel. Shortly you meet a well-made cart-track which turns north above the chapel. Climb it until you meet a path to the right signposted to Grand Som (the track itself carries on to Col de la Ruchère and Petit Som). Take the path; tree roots make an elaborate stairway as you climb, and the path is marked at intervals with red arrows. On the right, under a cleft of rock, is a spring dated 1778. Beyond it the path hairpins and approaches a massive cliff; at the top of the hairpin is a signpost to La Correrie and, to the left, Grand Som.

Follow the path to Grand Som through sycamore trees and then steeply up a broad gully towards a rock surmounted by a cross. Behind you, across a scree slope, are steep Alpine meadows; and in the cliffs, you may see a flock of choucas wheeling.

Pass a signpost on the left to Col de la Ruchère par Le Pas du Loup and continue straight ahead towards the cliff. The path, which is indicated by yellow marks on the rocks, curves towards the NE and emerges from the woods into a high alpine meadow loud with the bells of cattle. It curves past a shepherd's hut and a spring, and approaches a signpost to Grand Som and, to the west, Col de Lechaud and Petit Som. At a further signpost turn sharp right and climb steeply upwards towards a gully. There are fine views from here, down to Le Granier and across to the hills beyond the *zone de silence*. When you reach the gully, look for the blue and yellow arrows marking the path. The rocks are polished smooth, and could be treacherous in wet weather.

A junction in the track, marked by a signpost, offers alternative routes to the summit. To the left is the Sentier des Moutons, and, ahead, the path to Grand Som *par le sangle* (fork of path). The former is slightly further, but slightly less steep; follow it up across rocks until you meet a track across the grass where you turn right. The track leads up to the top of the ridge, from which opens up an astounding view east to Belledonne and NE to Mont Blanc. Far below on the valley floor are the hamlets of Les Arragons and St Phillibert.

The path turns southwards and leads somewhat awkwardly over rocks and scree along the eastern slope of the summit, and then pleasantly along the ridge towards the summit itself.

The descent is by the Pas de la Suiffière and the Col du Bachais. Take a path marked with blue arrows and blue and yellow waymarks which leads eastwards down a grassy slope studded with gentian. The path, which is much eroded, descends in hairpins and becomes rocky as the hill falls away; it curves round to the right, in the direction of the Dent de Crolles, and winds down through a steep gully where tiny wild rhododendrons and mountain orchids grow. At the foot of the gully the path turns sharp right under the cliffs and leads across a slope towards woods and, in the distance, the Dent de Crolles. It climbs fairly steeply, marked by waymarks on the rocks, until it reaches a gully on the right-hand side. Climb through this, and down a steep path, marked by yellow arrows, which leads to a scree slope. Far below can be seen the roofs of the monastery and in the SW, la Pinéa and Charmant Som. The path is clearly marked across the scree as it descends beneath a line of steep cliffs.

At the end of the cliff the path turns right to the SW and enters the woods. It leads clearly downhill to a sign indicating La Correrie and the monastery ahead, St-Pierre-de-Chartreuse to the left, and Grand Som behind. Follow down towards La Correrie; the path descends steeply through thick undergrowth and then hairpins westwards down a combe under trees. (The occasional short cut leads directly between hairpins – their use is not recommended, even though it takes longer than you might expect to climb downhill on hairpins.) Continue down until you reach a treetrunk with a sign on it indicating that the path ahead is *sans issue* (has no exit); the monastery is down to the right. From here the hairpins become steeper, and the path not so well made; after a brief, easy patch beneath a pine forest the way becomes rocky among a mass of broken tree trunks and needs to be searched out. At a fallen (in 1989) signpost marking La Correrie turn left down the unsignposted path to a wider track heading SW. Follow this to a signpost marked to La Correrie; here you rejoin the path taken from the monastery to La Correrie in Walk 15. It is possible to return to the start of the walk either direct to La Correrie to the left, or by way of the monastery, to the right; both involve a further 30 minutes walking.

Walk 17 Environs of Les Adrets

Map no	IGN 3334 est
Distance	5.5km (3.4 miles)
Ascent	138m (453ft)
Walking time	2$^1/_2$ hours
Grading	Easy (1)

This is a pleasant low level walk rising from 750m to 896m (2,460ft to 2,940ft), taking in some pretty villages and a notorious castle – the Maison Forte des Adrets – and hostelry – the Auberge des Adrets. Despite the fact that it is one of the most modest of the castles in the Dauphiné, the Maison Forte, as we shall see, is rich in legend and history, and the Auberge became famous as the title of a nineteenth century melodrama by Alexander Dumas.

Les Adrets signifies a settlement on a south-facing slope; and the village of some 400 inhabitants is prettily set on a hillside above the Ruisseau des Adrets.

Take the A41 from Grenoble to Brignoud; then the D523 to Froges and finally the D250 to les Adrets.

The Walk

The walk starts by the church, which is enriched by some fine woodwork in the apse, a fifteenth century Christ on the Rood, a somewhat garish eighteenth century madonna and child, and an ancient pew just inside the door. On the north wall of the tower are two clocks, the lower having only one hand in the medieval fashion: needless to say, they tell different times and one strikes two minutes after the other. An inhabitant who was asked why said that he didn't know, it had always been like that. In fact, it is a habit of many of the churches in the region to strike the hour twice!

Take the little road which heads east on the south side of the church, noting the immense wall on the left and the tiny dormer windows and massive eaves of the house on the right. Beyond the house is a wall with a pantiled roof and a massive gateway, for all the world like the enclosure of a

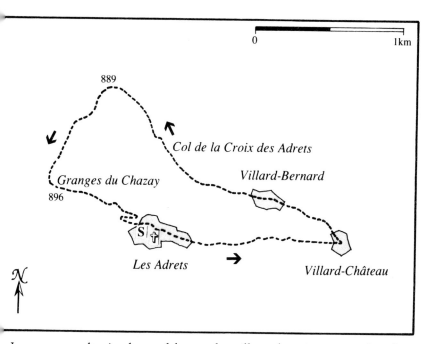

Japanese temple. As the road leaves the village there is a notice board indicating walks in the area. Take the gravel track leading alongside the hill beneath the cemetery: far to the right can be seen the Chaîne de Belledonne above the Lac de Crop (Walk 18); and on the hill to the SW the harsh concrete of the ski resort of Prapoutel. The track climbs steeply between lush meadows and walnut trees towards Villard Château: ignore the track leading uphill towards a house as the track makes a double bend by a farm, and continue between thick hedges to meet a road opposite a fountain, where you turn right.

A hundred metres along the road, on a knoll on the right-hand side, is La Maison Forte du Baron des Adrets. Now it seems little more than a large house, its peaceful air emphasised by the wisteria growing around the window; the thickness of its walls and a little barred window just by the door give the only clues to its turbulent past. It was, in fact, the castle of François de Beaumont, Baron des Adrets, one of the cruellest leaders in the wars of religion. It formed part of a defensive chain built by the Dauphins to stop the incursions of the Dukes of Savoie. According to local legend there are secret chambers beneath the castle, whose doors shut to entomb any hapless explorer who chances upon them; and cows disappear into holes suddenly opening up in the meadows beneath the ramparts. Like many of the leaders

93

of those times, François would back whatever side was winning; and he changed allegiance more often than the Vicar of Bray – to the discomfiture of his vassals.

Opposite the gate of the castle is a fountain. Take the green track leading left just past the fountain parallel with the road, and cross the road between two modern houses to take the cart-track heading north towards Les Prés Communaux. Walnut trees and beehives are in the field to the right; and a modern flat-roofed chalet to the left. Pass a dry stone wall and a house with a pretty garden to approach the road through a grassy courtyard surrounded by ancient farm buildings. There is a cross beneath a pine tree at the point where you meet the road; and a fountain opposite.

Turn left to walk down the metalled road towards Villard-Bernard. On the left is a woodbarn, holding freshly cut pine for fence posts; on the right, a curious little model house on a house roof. Pass an orchard, ignoring the road to the right, and continue to reach an ancient barn where the road turns back on itself in a hairpin. Here continue straight ahead west on a little road between two buildings marked by a 2m and 10 tonnes restriction sign. Beyond is a picturesque hamlet, alive with flowers in baskets; in a courtyard to the left, in the wall of a barn, is an ancient bread oven with its fire-back dated 1767 and implements hanging on the wall; in the house opposite can be bought the local honey. Further up through the hamlet is another oven just past a fountain. Ancient barns vie with modern chalets; one barn has a cross built into its lintel.

The road leaves the hamlet and, becoming a gravel track shaded with large ash trees, leads uphill towards the Col de la Croix des Adrets 871m (2,858ft). Below to the left is the village of Les Adrets; half left is the valley of the Isère. At the col are two pretty barns; to the right a valley leads down towards Hurtières; and the col is marked by a rude cross beside one of the barns.

Take the path leading uphill immediately opposite the barns, and take the left fork (the footpath to the right leads to Hurtières). Take the next track on the right, before you reach a little wood, and follow it slightly downhill, round the contours. Below you is the village of Hurtières, and beyond it the Crêt de la Couan 879m (2,884ft). The track begins to climb, passing a barn, and curves left into the wood to head SE around the Crêt du Chazay 953m (3,127ft). Just past the barn there is a junction; take the lower (right-hand) track to head slightly downhill through gloomy fir trees. Pass a spring on the left-hand side of the track, beside which is a wooden bench. Beyond there is a line of red marks heading uphill on trees, marking the edge of a parcel of forest. Just beyond the path splits again; take the higher of the two paths to reach, beyond thick and gloomy trees, a pasture and the Granges du Chazay,

Les Adrets

two barns, one ruined, at 896m (2,940ft) – the highest point on the walk.

From here turn left, between the barns, to skirt the edge of the pasture and re-enter the woods heading west. The path leads through a mixed forest of oak, beech and fir, to reach a stile and descend steeply to a cattle trough and then through trees to leave the woods by a pasture. The path here can be wet underfoot, even in dry weather.

The path leads NE across the pastures to reach the road from Col de la Croix des Adrets to les Adrets. Make your way down to the village; there is a short cut through steep banks about 100m to the right of the point where you reached the road; but it is not recommended in wet weather.

The Auberge des Adrets provides a comfortable finishing point. It has a scrubbed wooden floor and old photographs of the village as it was in the nineteenth century, together with skiing souvenirs, vast arrangements of dried flowers, a badger's pelt, a Thai fan, and other trophies of the chase. There is little feeling of melodrama in the inn today; but perhaps this diverse collection of objects reflects the Baron's eclecticism as he switched from one allegiance to another in order to keep his skin.

Walk 18   Lac de Crop

Map no	IGN 3334 est
Distance	10km (6.2 miles)
Ascent	638m (2,093ft)
Walking time	5 hours
Grading	Difficult (5)

The Lac de Crop 1,906m (6,253ft) is a sombre sheet of water hemmed in by the ragged mountains and glacial screes of the high Alps; its pewter surface reflects eternal snow and scudding clouds; the jagged peaks of Le Grand Replomb are drowned in its depths. Yet the climb up to the lake is through rich forest and lush pastures where butterflies dance and Alpine flowers flourish; and the ridge beneath the lake is traversed by a spectacular balcon path. The stiff climb is well rewarded, both by variety, and by the views from the lake.

Leave via the A41 from Grenoble to Brignoud, then the D528 to a point 3km south of Prabert where electricity cables cross the road at its junction with the GR549. There is a parking place on the right-hand side, before the track downhill signposted to the Pont de la Betta.

The Walk

Follow the track, which forms part of the GR549 and is marked by white and red waymarks, down through mature pines, some of which have been drilled to produce resin.

At the Pont de la Betta 1,306m (4,285ft) the track curves right into the Forêt Communale de Laval; the stream falls prettily over rapids. Continue past a sign to the Pré Marcel and the Col des Mouilles, to another sign and a track leading off to the left southwards; a red arrow on a rock just up this path points to the Lac de Crop (the sign indicates Laval ahead along the forest track and the Col de Mouilles and Prabert behind).

The path leads steeply uphill south towards the massive wall of the Grand Replomb, Le Ferrouillet and Le Point du Sciallet. After some 300m it swings

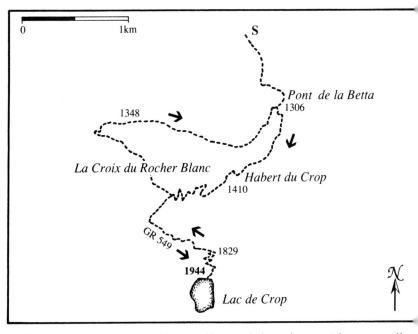

SW along the contours and is joined by a path from the east. There are well-spaced pine trees; and to the left of the path a rugged gully aptly named the Ravin de l'Avalanche. Far over to the north-west can be seen the Dent de Crolles in the Chartreuse.

The path passes a white and red waymark on a rock, and begins to climb again over humps, falling to a rivulet and veering SW to meet the swiftly flowing Ruisseau de Crop. Cross the stream by a well-made wooden bridge alongside the ruins of the Habert de Crop and follow its northern bank up a combe. Over to the left, on the opposite side of the valley, streams of water issue from the mountain below the lake (itself still invisible behind the hillside) and descend in long white cascades. These are the appropriately named Pisses du Crop. The peaked mountain ahead is the Montagne de Barlet 2,093m (6,867ft), which looms over the north-west of the lake.

The path climbs the combe in steep hairpins and enters a pine wood. Just before the further edge of the wood is a flat clearing with a fireplace which makes a pleasant picnic spot; here the path which we shall take on our descent leads north-west across the Croix du Rocher Blanc. Continue south-west uphill towards the edge of the wood and the ruins of the Deuxième Habert de Crop, just below the track. The Haberts, like sheilings in the Outer Hebrides, formed shelters for shepherds grazing their flocks on the summer pastures. Like sheilings, they are now open to the skies and given over to birds and rank weeds; but the summer pastures are rich as ever.

The path leads to a spectacular balcon, loud with the noise of falling waters, beneath the ridge and above the combe and the cascades of the Pisses du Crop. The balcon is narrow and well maintained, probably by Alpine troops; but the views downhill to the combe are not for those who suffer from vertigo. Across to the NNE is the resort of Prapoutel, its harsh lines softened by distance; the route of GR549 to Prapoutel is clearly visible across the slope beneath Le Jas des Lièvres, behind which are the jagged peaks of the Cime de la Jasse, 2,478m (8,130ft) and the Dent du Pra, 2,603m (8,540ft).

After a well-graded passage across a scree slope and a second smaller section of scree, the path meets a large notice painted on a rock '*Réserve de Chasse*', and begins to climb steeply in a series of twenty-four hairpins towards the moraine which dams in the lake. The lake is some 50m below the ridge; its surface reflects the steel grey and pewter of its surrounding; and even in high summer there is likely to be snow by the shore. Beyond, climbing up the scree slope to the south, is the continuation of GR549 to Lac Bleu 2,036m (6,680ft) and the Col de la Mine de Fer. For those with the time and the right equipment, this forms a superb walk through stark hills. Around are fiercely steep mountains, jagged rocks and slopes of scree. The French would probably describe a scene like this as '*jolie*', but the English words which come to mind are sombre or sublime.

Return down the hairpins and across the Alpages to the fireplace in the wood where the path leads NW across the Croix du Rocher Blanc. Take this path through trees and lush vegetation – a marked contrast to the environs of the lake – under a fallen tree and down steep hairpins. At the bottom of the hairpins you reach a track running along the contours to your left and right; behind you, on a tree, is an old notice marking a *réserve de chasse*. Turn left, and walk downhill to meet more steep hairpins leading down beside a crag. The path levels off and continues north-west: the trees here are mature; and there has been much working in the forest. At a meeting of tracks beside a rock there is a blue signpost marked to the Lac de Crop and the Refuge Jean Collet. Take the path on your right leading NNE, and follow the hairpins downhill. Forestry working has made it difficult to follow the path here; and you may find it necessary to leave it to meet, 100m down the slope, a forestry track heading east/west.

Turn east, and follow the track gently downhill along the contours. Your way is occasionally hindered by felled trees; there are yellow and red waymarks; and a sign on a tree to the right indicating the Col des Mouilles and that the Pont des Avoux is 30 minutes distant. Follow on down until you meet a landslip; here it is necessary to scramble up rocks to the right of the track to meet a new forestry road. Thirty minutes from the signpost you do indeed reach the Pont des Avoux; here there is a pretty cascade. The Pont de la Betta is a short step downhill, and the road some 5 minutes climb from there.

The village of Prabert is well worth a visit on your return, either by car, or along the footpath which leads parallel to the road. There is a tiny thirteenth century chapel dedicated to St Bernard with a stone floor and a simple romanesque arch. Wood is stacked against the west wall for the winter. From the churchyard you can look across to the Chaîne de Belledonne and the mountains surrounding the Lac de Crop. A sign by the road junction suggests walks in the area, and there is a pleasant café near the chapel with tables set in a garden under horse chestnut trees. Its simple menu offers omelettes (FF18), meat platters (FF26), *fromage blanc* (FF10) and *tarte aux myrtilles* (FF10). Simple and unpretentious, this is an excellent place to relax after a strenuous day's walking.

Walk 19   Col de Merdaret and Grand Rocher

Map no	IGN 3234 est
Distance	12km (7.5 miles)
Ascent	600m (1,969ft)
Walking time	4$^{1}/_{2}$ hours
Grading	Moderate (4)

This walk offers a steep climb through woods, which is followed by an easy ridge walk to a summit at 1,926m (6,319ft) with splendid views over Belledonne.

Follow the D280 north out of Theys to the signpost for Urplan. Take the second road on the right towards the Institut Médico-Pédagogique; at Le Rocharet take the right turn towards the Gorges du Replat. The road climbs in a series of steep hairpins through the Gorges and the Forêt des Ramiettes to the end of the metalled road beneath the Crêt du Trou, where you can park at 1,380m (4,528ft).

The Walk

Take the forest road heading south under the Crêt du Trou 1,463m (4,800ft), passing a track leading downhill to the right and continuing round along the contours. The path is surfaced for a spell in green broken glass, perhaps not to encourage Dick Whittington but to discourage cars. To the west are views of the Dent de Crolles and Chamechaude in the Chartreuse. Pass a signpost to Les Merdarets; either take the steep path indicated uphill, or continue along the forest road round a hairpin, to reach the Cabane Forestière, a mountain hut with a stove, a raised sleeping platform and rough wood furniture. From here a path is shown on the map leading SSW to the Chalet de Ramiettes and the Col de Merdaret. From the Chalet des Ramiettes, however, the path becomes very boggy; and it is better to take the higher path to the Col de Merdaret.

To do so, follow the mountain track from the Cabane Forestière around the next hairpin and uphill NE to a crossroads; here take the track leading

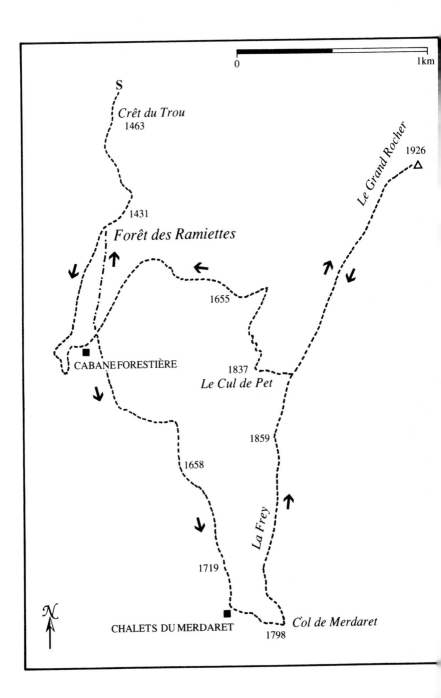

S

Crêt du Trou
1463

Le Grand Rocher
1926 △

1431

Forêt des Ramiettes

1655

CABANE FORESTIÈRE

1837
Le Cul de Pet

1859

1658

La Frey

1719

CHALETS DU MERDARET
1798
Col de Merdaret

N

0   1km

right SSE and climbing moderately steeply through woods. There are many wild raspberries in the woods, and wide views to the Lac de Crop.

The path becomes overgrown and difficult underfoot. It swings eastwards to meet a forest road; turn right to climb steeply east towards a signpost to Merdaret. Follow the indicated track south; it is well made and keeps to the contours, giving superb views downhill to Theys and across the River Isère to the Chartreuse, and southwards to the northern hills of the Vercors. The path leads steadily upwards, offering bilberries galore; as it leaves the woods it levels off to give a view of the ridge and of the head of a ski-lift.

Ford a little stream, and come through a gate in the fence to a prairie in which stands the Chalet du Merdaret. Take the higher of the two paths across the pasture; then leave it to climb east to the col 1,798m (5,899ft). There are fine views across to the Crêt du Boeuf 1,822m (5,978ft) and La Grande Roche 2,344m (7,690ft). The path leads round the left-hand side of a little summit, then across a prairie along the ridge; it is marked by yellow and red waymarks and despite a slight upwards gradient is very easy walking.

There are a lot of cattle here wearing musical cowbells; and you may meet a bull: if so, it is possible to walk just outside the fence marking off the ridge. Far below in the valley is the village of La Bourjat beside a reservoir. The path passes a slope with dwarf rhododendrons, then leaves the summit ridge and continues north along the eastern slopes to pass a little dew pond, the mud in it almost red. You may meet mountain bikes here; and there is likely to be a good number of walkers – it is an easy ridge walk from the Crêt du Poulet (Walk 20). The path crosses to the other side of the ridge and approaches the cross at the summit of Le Grand Rocher 1,926m (6,319ft).

To return, walk back south along the eastern side of the ridge towards le Cul de Pet until you see a little pond beneath you, Le Leatel Lac, below which is a bend in the forest track by the exposed rock of a cutting. Continue along the ridge until you meet a path which hairpins downhill towards Le Leatel Lac in a treeless combe, at the bottom of which are some ruins. Make your way to the ruins and then turn ESE towards a wood. The path leads down the right-hand side of the combe to enter the wood, from which it descends steeply to meet a grassy forest track by a tree to which is nailed a plastic forestry notice on which is printed the number 20. Turn right to follow the grassy track downhill to meet the mountain track by the exposed rock which you saw from the ridge. Continue WNW on the right fork of the hairpin; after some 100m the track swings round SSW to reach, after about $^3/_4$km, the crossroads above the Cabane Forestière. Turn right, and follow the track north through the trees to rejoin the forest road you took on your ascent and return to the metalled road below the Crêt du Trou.

Walk 20   Crêt du Poulet

Map no	IGN 3234 est
Distance	6km (3.7 miles)
Ascent	330m (1,083ft)
Walking time	2 hours
Grading	Easy (2)

The walk begins at the road end where you left your car at the start of Walk 19. Drive along the track signposted to Crêt du Poulet – a well-made forestry track leading slightly uphill through a thick forest. In due course the wood thins down to the left giving views across the valley. Ignore a path heading steeply uphill to the right. After some 2.5km you reach a path leading up to the right signposted to Pierre Roubet (yellow waymarks) and Col de Merdaret (yellow and red waymarks); and to the right Crêt Luisard 1 hour 30 minutes; Crêt du Poulet 1 hour 40 minutes; Chalet de Pierre Roubet 30 minutes; Lac de la Belle Aiguette 1 hour 15 minutes.

The Walk

Follow the well-made forestry track uphill towards the Chalet de Pierre Roubet. The track, which is marked by yellow and red waymarks on stones, leads uphill quite steeply between trees. Note the occasional drainage channel made by a treetrunk slanted diagonally across the track. After a few hundred metres the track bears to the right and the gradient slackens. Pass through the electric fence across the track; a notice on the left-hand side summarises the French country code:

Promeneurs vous allez rencontrer des animaux en liberté. Respectez leurs habitudes pour faciliter le travail des bergers. Fermez les barrières des enclos après votre passage. Tenez votre chien en laisse. N'abandonnez pas verre, boites de conserves, plastiques dangereux pour les animaux. Merci. Motos interdites du premier mai au 30 octobre.

Follow the grassy track up to the Chalet de Pierre Roubet, a somewhat austere building in private ownership, set in a pleasant meadow. We asked

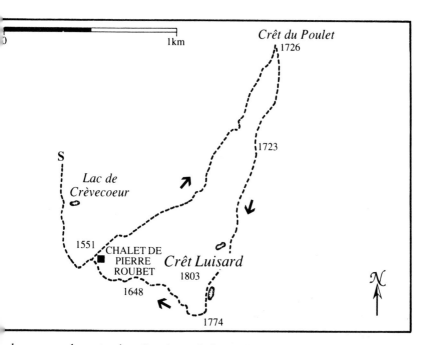

Crêt du Poulet 1726

1723

S

Lac de Crèvecoeur

1551

CHALET DE PIERRE ROUBET

Crêt Luisard 1803

1648

1774

1km

the owner, who arrived in a Landrover laden with provisions for the weekend, who Pierre Roubet was; he had no idea! Over one of the doors is a motto 'Si tu es un homme tu admireras mon paysage; si tu es un âne tu marqueras ton passage!' (If you are a man, you will remark my pasture; if you are an ass, you will mark your passing.) By the chalet is a fountain of sweet-tasting water, and there is a cross on the hillside above it to the left. Westwards is a fine view to the Chartreuse.

While the notice board at the start of the walk suggested that it might take half an hour to reach the chalet, it is possible to reach it in half that time if you do not linger: the indications of time on signposts in the area generally give a good deal of leeway.

Climb up the hill leaving the chalet on your right towards a signpost at the entrance to the wood. The signpost marks a path to the left to the Crêt du Poulet (30 minutes), and to the right Le Grand Rocher (1 hour) and Col de Merdaret. Take the left path NE towards the Crêt du Poulet; the path is clearly defined as it enters the wood, passing through scattered trees and marked by yellow and red waymarks. It leads through a gap in an electric fence and into the wood proper, climbing steadily uphill; a magnificent panorama opens to the left as you climb.

The path crosses a little meadow, then re-enters the wood, passing a modern *source captée* to the left and climbing up a hairpin to follow the line of a new road on the left-hand side. This has been recently built to open up the area for cross country skiing; neither it nor the Refuge du Crêt du Poulet are marked on the map. The path climbs parallel to the road; then crosses it, still heading NE, to reach a prairie where it levels out to meet a rough earthen track. A notice on a tree marks the Refuge du Crêt du Poulet; here it is possible to buy drinks, tarts, *fromage blanc*, as well as a full meal. To the left is the top of a ski-lift. The refuge is at the far end of the meadow; it has twenty-three beds in an upstairs dormitory. There is a menu at FF75 and breakfast is FF20. The tarts and gateaux, which are home-made, are delicious and would make the walk to the chalet worthwhile even if the views were hidden in fog. The chalet is open in the summer until about 15 September depending on the number of clients; in the winter it is used by voluntary organisations.

Head back from the chalet to climb southwards along the ridge on the path signposted to Le Grand Rocher (1 hour 30 minutes). The path leads slightly uphill through a pasture among sparse trees; continue straight ahead on a waymarked path where the cart track turns right, passing a pond and then a little lake with a knoll above it – the Lac de la Belle Aiguette. Continue along the ridge to reach a second weedy lake on the right of the track. About 100m beyond the southern end of the lake the path veers westwards towards a col at 1,774m (5,820ft) below the Crêt Luisard. This is the highest point of the walk.

Cross the col and walk westwards, slightly downhill, until you meet a path heading steeply downhill SW between scattered pine trees. From here a grassy track – not waymarked – leads directly downhill westwards over a pasture and towards a combe. Keep to the right-hand side of the combe as you descend NNW to pick up a path heading steeply downhill between trees. The path passes through a fence by a cattle trough made out of a brown bath, and continues downhill, more clearly defined now, alongside a small stream formed by the overflow. From this point is is possible to see the cross on the hill above the chalet. Pass a second cattle trough on the left, down to the signpost at the entrance of the wood above the chalet; and from this point retrace your steps to the start of the walk.

Walk 20A

It is possible to combine Walks 19 and 20 to form a longer walk of some 15km (10 miles). From the Grand Rocher (Walk 19) continue northwards along the ridge to reach the Lac de Séchident 1,849m (6,066ft) and the col at 1,774m (5,820ft) below the Crêt Luisard from which you descended in Walk

20. From here, either descend as in Walk 20 to the Chalet de Pierre Roubet, or continue along the ridge past the Lac de la Belle Aiguette to reach the Refuge du Crêt du Poulet and descend via Walk 20 in reverse. From the signpost at the start of Walk 20, take the forestry track southwards to the start of Walk 19.

Walk 21   Lac Achard

Map no	IGN 3335 ouest
Distance	6.25km (3.9 miles)
Ascent	167m (548ft)
Walking time	$2^1/_4$ hours
Grading	Easy (2)

This is a pleasant short stroll, suitable for an evening or a Sunday afternoon, to one of the most picturesque lakes in Belledonne. Despite the fact that it is at the centre of a popular skiing area, the lake is so situated in a hollow of the mountains that it is hardly possible to see any ski-lifts from it, and the contrast between the business of the resort and the tranquillity of the lake could hardly be more marked. But the area is significant as one of the cradles of the Alpine tourist industry. Here, at Roche Béranger, dwelt a famous hermit, Père Tasse, who welcomed everyone to his cell and opened up the mountains to those who loved them. It is said that the emblem of Chamrousse, the bear, derives from the fact that Père Tasse wrestled with bears when living alone in what was then a wilderness.

From Station de Chamrousse, take the D524 from Grenoble and thereafter D111 from Uriage-les-Bains to the commercial centre of Roche Béranger.

The Walk

Leave the village of Roche Béranger and walk south towards the pistes; for those who wish to try their luck at mountain biking there is a hire shop in the terrace on the left (FF75 per day). Take the road downhill towards the children's village of Bachat Bouloud and across a bridge. To the left, slightly up the hill, is a hut hiring Yamaha *Scooters de neige*: not particularly suitable for high summer despite the fact that snow is visible on the high peaks. Follow the hairpin uphill to reach a car park: at its eastern end is a path signposted to Lac Achard and La Lauze. The path leads uphill through rocks; across the valley to the SE are the great ramparts of the Rocher de l'Homme, and ahead can be seen the summit of a *télésiège* – the Télésiège des Lacs Achard.

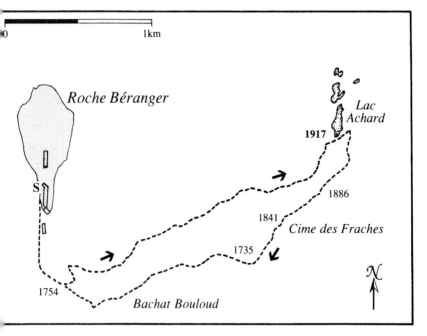

Roche Béranger

Lac Achard

1917

1886

Cime des Fraches

1841

1735

1754

Bachat Bouloud

0   1km

S

N

The path is marked with yellow waymarks, and climbs gently through scattered pine trees to reach a signpost to 'Lac Achard 1 hour 15 minutes'. To indicate distances in time rather than kilometres can be good for morale – the figures are smaller and sometimes you can beat the suggested time. We passed the signpost at 5.15pm and determined to see whether or not we could beat the clock.

Pass under a *télésiège*, pausing to look at the eternal snows of Belledonne: the landscape here is far more rugged than the Vercors, and more rugged even than the Chartreuse. The path gradually becomes rockier as you climb to 1,800m (5,906ft) through La Lauze. Beneath you to the SSE is the meadow of L'Arselle bounded by the Forêt Communale de Séchilienne; and ahead to the east, above the narrow valley of the Ruisseau de Salinière, (down which you will return) are the sheer cliffs and living rocks of Le Grand Sorbier 2,525m (8,287ft).

The path climbs steeply between rocks; choucas wheel in the cliffs above. It becomes more level by a signpost to Lac Achard, and there is a downhill stretch through sweet-smelling grasses to more rocks marked with a yellow waymark. A tooth-like rock appears ahead of you; and there are Alpine rhododendrons by the side of the path – nothing like the massive Himalayan bushes which have colonised the western highlands of Scotland, but dwarf bushes entirely fitted to their surroundings: the bonsai trees of the French Alps.

Climb up a steep cliff, perhaps meeting a group of children from one of the summer camps which are held in the Bachat Bouloud. Beyond is a brook, and then Lac Achard, at 1,917m (6,289ft) beautifully set in a horseshoe of hills some 100m higher than the lake itself – the Col de l'Infernet to the right, and the Rocher de la Perche ahead to the north. The time of ascent was 1 hour – somewhat better than the signpost led us to suppose.

The descent takes you beneath the Cime des Fraches 1,942m (6,371ft) and along the brook which flows from Lac Achard – Le Ruisseau de Salinière. The path begins at a signpost 100m from the southern shore of the lake and leads south, passing steep rocks to the left. Walk towards a pole, noting the Dent d'Alexandre 1,553m (5,095ft) to the east, and follow the path downhill past white waymarks. On a clear day it is possible to make out the southern Vercors SSW from here, with the strange flat-topped Mont Aiguille rising sheer from the surrounding hills. The grassland here is studded with succulents, yellow gentians and dwarf rhododendrons; and dragonflies dart above little pools.

Take the path down along the left-hand side of a ravine and into thicker trees where it broadens to reach a clearing. Follow down past an arrow (white painted on red) to cross the Ruisseau de Salinière. A tree has fallen across the stream and could serve as a bridge in spring or autumn; but in summer the stream is likely to be dry.

The path leads NE from the stream, across a little meadow and then into a wood of well-spaced trees and along the edge of further meadows. It crosses a stream on a bridge of treetrunks and, after another bridge, reaches a signpost to Bachat Bouloud, L'Astragale 2km 100m and L'Arselle 1km. Follow the wide gravel path leading through woods to Bachat Bouloud.

Pass under the Télésiège des Clairières to approach a barrier in the road; beyond, on a tree, is a notice indicating the places where the various groups of children in the village are to rendezvous. We noted, smugly, the signpost to Lac Achard '$1^1/_2$ hours'.

Follow past the chalets of the village, taking the right-hand turn towards Roche Béranger, to meet the bridge near the start of the walk about 5 minutes up the road. The village has none of the charms of those in the Vercors or Chartreuse, but is typical of modern ski resorts and has a number of bar restaurants where you can get a meal or a drink to celebrate completing the walk more quickly than the signposts had led you to suppose.

Walk 22   La Cascade de l'Oursière

Map no	IGN 3335 Ouest
Distance	7.25km (4.5 miles)
Ascent	387m (1,270ft)
Walking time	$2^{1}/_{2}$ hours
Grading	Moderate (3)

This short though slightly stiff walk leads to the biggest and most impressive waterfall in Belledonne – a land of cascades. The waterfall is 92m (302ft) high, and is divided by rocks into two separate cascades. Below it are the ruins of a nineteenth century chalet, and a convenient picnic place.

Travel on the D111 from Grenoble to Chamrousse 6km (4 miles) from St-Martin-d'Uriage.

The Walk

The walk begins by the hotel at Les Seiglières. Walk eastwards around a bend in the D111 to a forest road which leads off to the left and follows below the line of the road. A red notice on a tree to the left warns you that you are in a hunting reserve and should keep your dog on a lead. The path trends gently downhill through a sweet-smelling pine forest. Half left through the trees are the jagged peaks of Le Grand Colon 2,394m (7,854ft); the track narrows and climbs uphill past an orange arrow to meet a forestry track. Turn left. After some 200m the track divides. Take the left-hand track signposted to Clot des Vernes and L'Oursière, 1 hour 30 minutes. The track leads slightly downhill towards a little stream; a sign on the right indicates that you are in the Forêt Communale de St Martin d'Uriage. Ford the stream – the Ruisseau des Pourrettes – and follow the main track NE slightly downhill through the trees, ignoring the tracks leading off SE to the right.

The path curves round to the right; the ground falls away steeply to the left, and a waterfall is visible below you. Above you, through the trees, are the ragged peaks of the mountains and a waterfall tumbling from the Pic Chauvin in the appropriately named Ravin du Grand Canal.

111

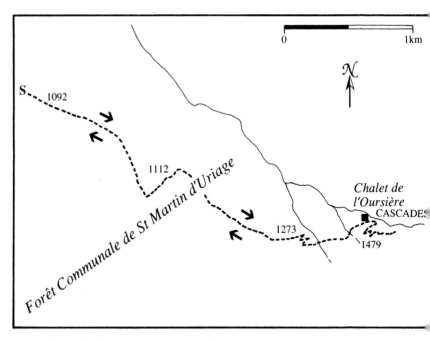

The track becomes a footpath and begins to climb between broad-leaved trees; ford a little stream – a good place to fill your water bottle – at 1,250m (4,101ft). Looking back to the NW are massive cliffs and, far below, the villages of La Chênevas and Les Cornets. Everywhere now is the sound of rushing water. Round a bend to approach a substantial torrent; with care it is possible to ford this, although it could prove difficult after rain.

The path approaches a ravine; take the diversion, marked by a red arrow on a rock, which hairpins back up the hill. After some 200m you will come across a tricky passage where the path has fallen away into the ravine; the path leads down into the ravine and the way across is marked by another red arrow. Further up the gully is a substantial torrent; but it disappears into the rocks above the crossing place – at least in high summer.

Scramble up the other side of the gully; the path is marked by red arrows and crosses another torrent with a waterfall above. From here the path becomes easier and passes through a pine wood to reach the ruins of a chalet and shortly afterwards you arrive at the Cascade de l'Oursière (the Waterfall of the Brown Bear), where the Ruisseau de Doménon falls 300ft down the mountainside.

Retrace your steps from the cascade. There is an alternative route across the ravine: just before you reach the ravine, take the path which leads off in hairpins downhill to the right. This crosses the gully and zigzags up the other side to meet the path by which you ascended just by the red arrow marking the diversion uphill. After fording the Ruisseau des Pourrettes, return to Les Seiglières along the forest track – the Chemin de la Gâte – and along the D111 westwards to the hotel.

Walk 23   Le Rosay and Gorges de la Sarenne

Map no	IGN 3335 est
Distance	10km (6.2 miles)
Ascent	Negligible; some steep sections
Walking time	3 hours
Grading	Easy (2)

This is an easy walk through the spectacular gorge of the River Sarenne below Huez, and around the pastures of the Montagne de l'Homme.

Travel on the D211 from Le Bourg-d'Oisans to La Garde; thence take the D211a to Armentier and Le Haut. Finally, take the minor road uphill to the hamlet of Maronne.

The Walk

The walk starts opposite the Hôtel La Forêt de Maronne. Take the minor road north towards Le Rosay, passing through the pretty hamlet of Maronne; below and behind you is the thick Forêt de Maronne, and above you the top of a *télésiège*. To the NNW is the town of Huez, and underneath is a waterfall. Pass a path to your right signposted to the Col de Maronne; you will come down this on your return. Above you on the right is the Montagne de l'Homme 2,176m (7,139ft).

Take the lower road as you enter Le Rosay, a pretty hamlet with flower boxes on the windowsills and a tiny chapel; there is a holy water stoup and carved cross with the IHS monogram outside, and a statue of the Virgin by the altar. From here follow the signpost to Huez and Besse along the route, marked with white and red waymarks, of GR54.

The path leads gently downhill through rowan trees; autumn crocuses stud the meadows even at the height of summer. The landscape is delightfully picturesque apart from the raw concrete buildings of Alpe-d'Huez – here it is inadvisable to 'lift up thine eyes unto the hills'! At the end of the meadow the path reaches rocks and passes by a ruined gateway to descend the cliff towards the Sarenne in steep hairpins. The path is not suitable for those

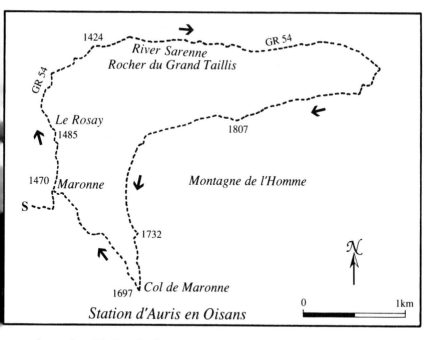

1424
→
GR 54
River Sarenne
Rocher du Grand Taillis
GR 54
1807
Le Rosay
↑ 1485
←
1470 Maronne
↓
Montagne de l'Homme
S
1732
↖
1697 Col de Maronne
N
↑
0   1km
Station d'Auris en Oisans

without a head for heights but it is nevertheless very well made – some of the hairpins are cambered. The path crosses a scree and reaches a bridge over the river – the Pont Romain. A jogging track leads upstream on the left bank of the river; but the path crosses to the other bank of the river.

Ignore the Chemin des Pêcheurs which follows immediately by the bank of the river, and walk slightly uphill to meet a path running left and right parallel with the river. The path has been laid out with a typical thoroughness to form an exercise track – hectoring notices tell you to perform vigorous exercises of one kind or another every 100m. On the left-hand side of the track are the ruins of a mill, where you are instructed to lean against a balk of wood and lift yourself five times if you are *familles* and ten times if you are *sportif*, and then walk, breathing heavily, to the next station, where there is a large ladder to be climbed. If you wish to keep your stamina for the walk, and the subsequent glass in the Hôtel La Forêt de Maronne you will ignore these instructions and pass through the obstacles as rapidly as possible. At Point 11 turn right to join a little road leading to the foot of a *télésiège* by the Cascade de Rieu Nay. Above you, on the crest of a steep hill, are the buildings of a *Club Hippique*.

Just past the *télésiège* the track forks. Take the upper fork and follow the rough road about 100m to a waymark. From here the track climbs gently and without much effort to pass under another *télésiège*. There is a profusion of rosebay willowherb and ash trees, and snapdragon in the undergrowth.

The track approaches close to the stream and passes besides a massive fall of rocks on the opposite bank under the Roche des Darances. From here it passes through a pleasant meadow, and by some substantial ruins – the ruins of Combe Haute to reach the foot of yet another *télésiège* – the Télésiège Chervet – which rises from 1,550m to 2,250m (5,085ft to 7,382ft). Here there is a restaurant – La Combe Haute – which is open in summer.

The track crosses the river on a broad bridge, and continues up the valley on the left bank of the river, passing through a narrow defile under the Roche des Darances and past another substantial rock fall. Beyond the defile the landscape opens out into the Combe Chave – a beautiful open valley with a stream rushing down towards the River Sarenne. A bridge crosses the river by a signpost to Huez, to the Col de Sarenne, and SE uphill, to the Col de Cluy 1,801m (5,909ft) and les Cours.

From the bridge take the earthen track uphill to the SW. The track passes some ruins and swings round to the right between the Roche des Darances and the Montagne de l'Homme. The meadow is studded with crocuses; and there is a sheep pen to the right of the track. Here the path levels and passes across a plateau at about the same height as Huez; there are fine views from here of the mountains surrounding Huez and of the deep gorge of the Sarenne; the scree above the gorges appears almost green. Clearly visible to the north is the airstrip of Alpe d'Huez; and small aircraft may be taking off and landing on pleasure flights. Beyond the town of Huez you can see the Grand Pic de Belledonne and the Croix de Belledonne.

Pass a large orange notice '*Retour Alpe-d'Huez* ' and continue along the track, above a ski resort at the head of the Télésiège des Gorges de Sarenne and the foot of the Télésiège Double de Fontfroide. The track leads around the contours and offers very easy walking. After about a kilometre it swings around to the right and begins to descend southwards. Far below to the right can be seen the hotel at the start of the walk, and ahead, due south, the glaciers of the Massif des Ecrins. The flora becomes more prolific as the track descends, and there are many yellow gentians by the side of the track.

Just before the col is a newly constructed *télésiège* leading to Signal de l'Homme; a path leads from the col 1,697m (5,568ft) to Station d'Auris-en-Oisans, where it is possible to hire ponies to carry your picnic and your children (FF50 for three hours, including paniers). Your path, however, turns right, passing the bottom of the ski-lift to head NE towards Maronne. Note the contrast between the old chalet on the left-hand side of the path as you begin to descend, losing its rusty roof and earth coloured walls in the hillside,

A Chalet at Le Rosay

and the new steel and white plastic *télésiège*, which can take a maximum of 2,000 people per hour 1,350m (4,429ft) at a speed of 2.25m (7ft) per second.

The path leads steeply downhill NW between two shoulders of hills and passes a wood on the left-hand side to rejoin the road from Maronne to Le Rosay at the signpost to Col de Maronne.

Walk 24   Lac Blanc and Refuge de la Fare

Map no	IGN 3335 est
Distance	8km (5 miles)
Descent	611m (2,005ft)
Walking time	4 hours
Grading	Difficult (6)

It is possible to start this walk either from the hotel at Maronne (*see* Walk 23) or from the *télécabine* shuttle to Alpe d'Huez at Huez.

The Walk

From the hotel at Maronne, take the road to the Pont Romain by way of Le Rosay where you will find a pleasant fountain just before a traditional stone-built house in course of being restored. At the top of the hamlet is a charming chapel in which mass was being celebrated as we passed – *see* Walk 23. Pass a barn to reach the track to the Pont Romain and the Gorge de la Sarenne.

Beyond the bridge – some 30 minutes' walk – turn left to follow the path west to Huez. Take the lower path at the fork, passing further stations on the jogging track. From here there are fine views of the cliffs above the River Sarenne down which the path to the Pont Romain zigzags; it is barely possible to see the course of the path. The village of Huez is reached some 45 minutes after leaving Maronne.

Huez is a mixture of traditional houses and modern infilling. Take the road opposite the beginning of the path from the Pont Romain to pass under a massive church built into the hillside and beside a fountain of ice cold water and reach the foot of the *télécabine*. This leads to the resort of Alpe d'Huez, and costs FF10 single; FF15 return; in summer it operates from 9am to 6.15pm. From it there are fine views of the valley and the town of Le Bourg d'Oisans; and on the road below – one of the more punishing legs of the *Tour de France* – are painted the names of riders.

L'Alpe d'Huez is a ski resort all year round; the buildings are functional and mostly ugly, and the whole place has a curiously temporary air, as though the

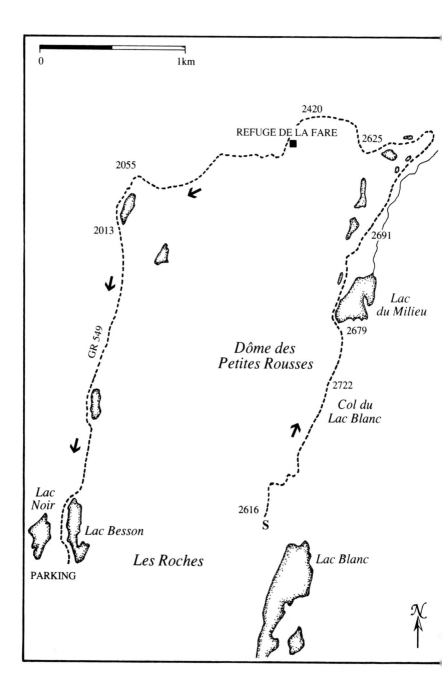

2420

REFUGE DE LA FARE

2625

2055

2013

GR 549

2691

Lac
du Milieu

2679

Dôme des
Petites Rousses

2722

Col du
Lac Blanc

2616

S

Lac
Noir

Lac Besson

Les Roches

Lac Blanc

PARKING

0   1km

N

Lac Blanc

Wild West had been transferred to the Dauphiné. There is indeed a Denver Saloon selling hot dogs, sandwiches, cocktails, beer and whiskey with an 'e'. For those who want other exercise than walking there is an open air swimming pool where topless sunbathing is permitted. The Télécabine des Grandes Rousses is at the top of the village, 10 minutes' walk from the *télécabine* from Huez. The ascent and descent costs FF42; there is, unfairly, no discount for those who wish only to ascend.

The *télécabine* climbs to the Pic Blanc; but leave it at the second station (*tronçon*), at 2,700m (8,858ft). Here the oxygen is markedly thinner than in the valley below. Below the station, to the SE, are the waters of Lac Blanc. Follow the well-made track northwards towards a col. Vegetation here is sparse and the landscape is bleak – there was once a glacier here and little grows. The rocks are heavily eroded and the mountainside below Le Pic Blanc is scarred with watercourses: a good deal of white water flows noisily down from the glaciers. The path ascends to reach the Col du Lac Blanc 2,722m (8,930ft) after some 25 minutes' walking.

At the col is a signpost, marking to the left (west) the Dome des Petites Rousses and, to the right, the Pic de la Pyramide and the Pic Bayle. Continue northwards by a cairn towards the Lac du Milieu, which is noted for the quality of its trout fishing. The path across the moraine is indicated by red

121

marks on the rocks; there are occasional flowers – small white anemonies, daisies, marguerites, little blue *clochettes* and other flowers of the high peaks.

The path approaches the SE corner of Lac du Milieu; despite the glaciers on the range to the right and the grey moraine it is very much less bleak here than on the other side of the col. A red arrow on a rock leads you past the corner of the lake and the path winds round the lake, marked by little cairns, red marks and the occasional red arrow.

Past a large rock with an arrow the view opens up to the left. Keep on the waymarked track past an amazingly clear pool; the rocks here are so clean it could almost be a sea-shore. Everywhere is the noise of falling meltwater from the glaciers and an incredibly clear blue light. The path winds between further lakes fed by massive cascades; a signpost by one of the larger lakes is marked back to Lac Blanc and the *téléphérique*.

The path descends to a sand beach the colour of ash; continue round it to a shelter where the path divides; the right-hand path is signposted to La Jasse, and the left-hand to L'Alpette. Take the left-hand path towards a signpost visible ahead; this indicates the Refuge de la Fare and Lac Besson. Look back at the glacier, which appears as though it could slide down the hill and engulf you. There are many glistening crystals in the rocks and sparse vegetation. The path winds over rough rocks towards another signpost and then to a cairn, from which it descends very steeply, marked by blue waymarks. The Alpine flowers are more profuse here.Some of the rocks are very slippery and great care is needed. As the path zigzags downhill it approaches a magnificent cascade.

The path snakes down the mountainside skirting a scree slope; keep off the dangerous sections marked off with orange and white tape. The Refuge de la Fare is at 2,300m (7,546ft); the walk here from the *télécabine* takes some 2 hours. At the refuge it is possible to buy refreshments and to stay the night; there are twenty-four beds.

From the refuge the path leads SE across a slope and towards a cliff; initially the gradient is more comfortable than earlier, but then the path descends steeply down hairpins. At one point a cord is hammered into the rock to assist your descent. From here the path approaches the foot of a cablecar; at the point where the path forks take the left-hand fork to climb down a substantial scree slope and between large rocks. There are superb views north to Belledonne.

Pass the cablecar station on the right, ignoring the welcoming road which runs downhill from this point, and follow the path uphill, underneath the wires and towards a large upright pole stuck in the rocks. Follow across more rocks to meet a grassy track leading up to a break between two banks. Turn sharp left before you reach the bank, and follow the blue waymarks along the side of the bank. At the end of the bank follow a newly made causeway; thence the path begins to descend west over broken rocky ground and through a wet meadow with bog cotton towards a tor. Skirt the side of the tor southwards; the lower station of the cablecar is immediately behind you and the higher station up the cliff to your left.

The path now leads south towards a lake – the Lac Faucille 2,063m (6,768ft) – and crosses a little dam at the end of the lake. It rises slightly along a meadow between two rocky outcrops and through a broken dry stone wall; a notice warns that '*Fouilles, Prospections et Extractions de Minéraux et Cristaux Interdites*' (It is forbidden to look for minerals and crystals). The walking here is beautifully comfortable after the scramble downhill.

Approach a second lake – the Lac Besson – across a grassy meadow; above it is a brown chalet, and beyond that the station for a *télécabine*. Cross the dam, and walk to the Chalet du Lac Besson, where it is possible to buy a wide variety of refreshments.

From here, walk down the road to L'Alpe d'Huez, or, if you can so arrange it, take a lift. We were fortunate in being offered a lift by a family we met in the Refuge de la Fare whose young children – aged six and eight – descended the hill like mountain goats.

If you started from Maronne, make your way to Huez by way of the cablecar or the path which runs downhill beneath it, and take the path from Huez by which you ascended from Maronne: this is signposted to the Gorges de la Sarenne. It is unlikely that, at this stage in the walk, you will wish to make use of the exercise park.

Walk 25   Barrage du Chambon, Cuculet and Mont-de-Lans

Map no	IGN 3435 ouest
Distance	6.5km (4 miles)
Ascent	203m (666ft)
Walking time	3 hours
Grading	Easy (2)

This is an easy walk giving fine views of the Lac du Chambon – a major hydro-electricity scheme – and the surrounding mountains and taking in the pretty village of Cuculet. The village of Le Chambon and the Chambon dam are a popular tourist spot; but the walk is very little frequented.

Le Chambon is situated on the N91 from le Bourg-d'Oisans to La Grave, 2.5km (1.5 miles) beyond Le-Freney-d'Oisans.

The Walk

From the Barrage du Chambon 1,044m (3,425ft) take the D213 south towards Mont-de-Lans. Eastwards along the lake can be seen the Pic de la Meije and the surrounding glaciers; the lake, which offers canoeing and sailing, is a vivid emerald green. On a lamp-post is the red and white waymark of a National GR – an alternative route for GR54 passes here and leads to Mont-de-Lans by a path leading off to the right after some 100m; the walk returns by way of this path. Shortly beyond this point a cart-track leads left downhill, signposted to 'Cuculet, 1 hour'. A notice warns against swimming and canoeing in the lake within 300m of the dam. On the opposite side of the lake is the village of Mizoën surmounted by a fine church.

The path leads pleasantly downhill over slippery schist, marked by the occasional blue waymark. Note the almost vertical strata of the rocks as you approach the point where the path turns back on itself to cross a little stream on an ugly concrete and steel bridge. From here the path swings north towards the lake and the Bois de Tardivière. At the fork just beyond a blue waymark take the upper path to follow hairpins uphill SW. The path, which is marked

124

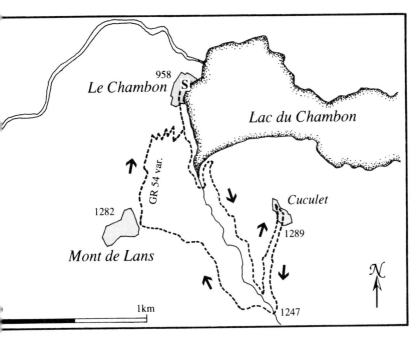

by blue waymarks, forms a balcon; it crosses a meadow and swings SSE along the eastern side of the valley. On the brow of the opposite hillside is a telecommunications station; and to the SE ahead is the peak of the Clot Gauthier.

After the meadows the path enters a forest, crosses a little stream and then takes a hairpin left up the hill and out on to another meadow. At this point we met four or five mountain bikers riding downhill at high speed, although the path is entirely unsuitable for them. The great area of bare stone on the opposite hillside shows the tortuous way in which the rocks have been folded. A dry stone wall on the side of the path protects an Alpine meadow now given over to scrub and small trees. Pass a pretty waterfall on the right-hand side of the track, beyond which the path climbs more steeply on hairpins to turn north through silver birch. As it leaves the wood it meets an *oratoire* containing a tiny cross of two sticks woven together with grasses.

The path, shaded with ash trees, crosses a green meadow bounded with dry stone walls to approach the village of Cuculet. To the west, across the valley and at the same level, is the village of Mont-de-Lans with its church steeple rising high above the rooftops. At the road turn left and walk towards the village, passing a new house on the right, and then a fountain. From the northern end of the village a path leads down through the Grand Bois to

125

Lac du Chambon from Cuculet

the head of Lac du Chambon; to the left, about 100 yds from the village, is a viewpoint on a pretty knoll which makes an attractive picnic place.

From the viewpoint retrace your steps to the top of the village and take the higher road southwards. There is an oak-studded door on a barn on the left-hand side of the road, and herbs drying on another doorway. Continue south on the metalled road, past the start of the path from Le Chambon and a postbox and village notice board. A warning sign alerts tourists to the dangers of straying on the banks of certain rivers whose water levels may rise suddenly as a result of hydro-electric operations.

Follow the minor road – which has virtually no traffic – downhill above meadows to meet a hairpin where it crosses the Ruisseau de la Pisse at 1,247m (4,091ft). From the bridge a path climbs south along the right bank of the river to the Cascade de la Pisse 1,550m (5,085ft); there are spectacular rapids beneath the bridge and on the river toward the cascade; and the cascade is well worth a diversion if you have time. Further down the road is a path leading left to Les Deux Alpes. Continue along the metalled road, passing a notice stating '*Commune de Mont-de-Lans: Ramassage d'escargots interdit sous peine de procès verbal* ' (It is forbidden to collect snails; penalty a summary fine).

Beyond the Lac du Chambon to the NE is the massif in which hides the

Plateau d'Emparis (Walk 26); one of the vertiginous roads into the plateau leads across the cliffs above the north bank of the lake and you may see cars passing slowly across the mountainside. The minor road joins the D213 just below the village of Mont-de-Lans.

Mont de Lans has some rather ugly modern chalets among older traditional buildings. The Bar La Tourelle has a 1950s decor of formica and steel; the church clock strikes the hours twice, like that of Les Adrets. The path follows the D213 for 250m north from the point where the minor road joins it; there are waymarks on the crash barrier at the roadside. A signpost on the right-hand side of the road indicates the path to Mizoën and Le Chambon; this is marked with blue waymarks, and descends steeply on well-made hairpins giving fine views of the Lac du Chambon and the surrounding mountains. The path crosses the road and continues downhill, marked by a signpost on an almost dead tree. It reaches the road above the Lac du Chambon about 100m from the barrage.

Walk 26   Plateau d'Emparis

Map no	IGN 3435 ouest
Distance	7.5km (4.6 miles)
Ascent	Negligible; some steep sections
Walking time	3 hours
Grading	Moderate (3)

The Plateau d'Emparis, or the Plateau de Paris as the IGN maps have it, is one of the more curious quarters of the French Alps. Set high among the peaks and glaciers of the Oisans, it has nevertheless the feel of the Scottish borders; and sheep graze on its vast grassy slopes. The Refuge du Fay have a well deserved reputation for the quality of its local cooking; we dined splendidly off home-made vegetable soup, belly pork with dumplings made to a secret recipe of locally gathered mountain herbs and the inevitable but delicious *fromage blanc*. And some travellers from the Midi, there to celebrate the feast of the Virgin with a brother who had a herd of sheep on the plateau, insisted on presenting us with a bottle of Châteauneuf du Pape 1986 on condition that we attended their feast and helped them eat the calf which they had driven up on to the Plateau, together with rosemary, firewood and enough wine to fill the Lac du Chambon, in an ancient Citroen van. But, quite apart from the hospitality of the place, the walks in the plateau and the views from it are well worth the effort of getting there.

For getting there is not easy. Take the D91 to Le-Freney-d'Oisans and Barrage du Chambon. There are two roads in – one from the village of Mizoën across the cliffs above the Lac du Chambon, and the other from the village of Besse on the D25. The road from Mizoën is metalled for a little way and has fewer hairpins; it does however require a very good head for heights. That from Besse is unmetalled and a single track with passing places beyond the Granges du Gay; it leads up the mountainside on vast hairpins and has a particularly difficult stretch over the Combe de Ruit. We were, nevertheless, reassured by the proprietor of the bar in Besse that the route was quite safe.

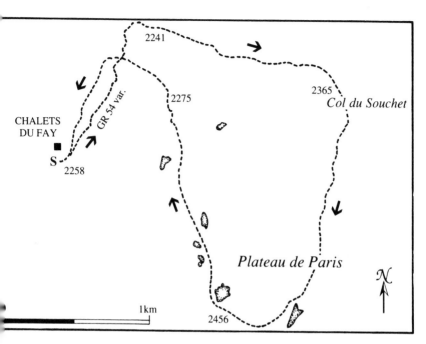

The Walk

The walk starts from the Refuge du Fay, from which there are fine views south to the Glacier de Mont de Lans and the Glacier de la Girose. Walk briefly northwards along the track towards a group of chalets; just before them there is a red and white waymark marking a path – an alternative route for the GR54 – downhill to the left. The path descends NNE past a blue signpost to the Refuge des Moutières and leads steadily downhill towards a chalet falling into ruins on the banks of a stream – the Rif Tort. Cross the stream and continue downstream on the other bank to meet a convergence of streams and paths in the midst of the plateau.

Take the path leading uphill SE to the right past a notice '*Commune de La Grave. Suivez les sentiers; Chiens Obligatoirement en Laisse* ' (Keep to the footpaths; Dogs must be kept on a leash). The path leads towards the eastern end of a line of rocky outcrops to the right and approaches a signpost marked to the Refuge Rif Tort, where there are beds, food and drink. Continue on the GR, crossing the course of a stream. The surrounding hills are rounded and grassy, and provide rich grazing for goats or sheep; but in the distance are high peaks and glaciers. The path climbs steadily uphill towards a col; down to the left is the Chalet de Paris; and ahead is the dramatic summit of the Pic de la

A walker above Lac Cristallin

Meije. The path continues east, then swings south to approach the Col du Souchet 2,365m (7,759ft).

Pass a small cairn on the left-hand side of the path. From here a number of paths head off to the right. Take the path heading 190° towards what looks like a massive boulder on the shoulder of a hill. On the other side of the valley of the Romanche can be seen the pistes on the Glacier du Mont de Lans.

The path leaves the route of the GR and heads gently downhill and between two shoulders of hill, then swings round to pass the large boulder on the left. The walking here is easy; the path is level, then leads slightly downhill towards Lac Lerié, passing a large beacon on a metal frame on its right-hand side. Lac Lerié is beautifully set among little hills and makes a fine picnic or camping place; the path skirts its northern shore.

From here the path leads west across ground which becomes increasingly broken. Climb up to a col above the lake, and take a small diversion left to the edge of the cliffs to see the magnificent view to the valley of the Romanche 1,300m (4,265ft) below. The path curves to the right, then west towards the shoulder of a hill between strata of limestone rich with rock plants. From here, it leads WNW towards Lac Noir, which looks sinister beneath a ridge surmounted by a line of five cairns. After the tranquillity of Lac Lerié it is aptly named.

The path passes a signpost to Lac Lerié and skirts the northern side of Lac Noir; it then swings north to pass a weather station used to monitor the depth of the snow. Follow it north past a series of dry lakes, to approach a cairn on the shoulder of the hill. There is a lot of exposed rock; and much quartz. From the cairn can be seen the valley of the Rif Tort, and the Chalets du Fay on the opposite hillside. Pass the cairn on the left, noting a further dry lake on the right, and continue NNW to reach Lac Cristallin; to the NE is Petit Lac Cristallin, which, unlike the other lakes in the area, has water even in high summer.

Make your way down the hillside heading generally northwards to a flat area between Lac Cristallin and Petit Lac Cristallin. There are some immense quartzes here, and evidence that the geologist's hammer has been at work. A signpost points back to the Lac Noir. From here the path is better defined, leading across rough rocks, down a short chimney, and over a scree slope. At the bottom of the scree is another signpost pointing back to Les Lacs.

The path leads clearly downhill towards the GR54; but at this point it is possible to take a short cut steeply downhill to the ruined chalet beside the crossing of the Rif Tort. From the chalet climb uphill west to meet another path leading south around the shoulder of the hill. This takes you back to the Refuge du Fay above the path which you took on the way down; just below the refuge a signpost on the track points to the 'Refuge du Fay 30m'.

Walk 27   La Grave to Les Terrasses and Ventelon

Map nos	IGN 3435 est and 3435 ouest
Distance	5km (3.1 miles)
Ascent	250m (820ft)
Walking time	2 hours
Grading	Easy (1)

This is a pleasant short walk, suitable for an evening, taking in two settlements and the village of La Grave. La Grave is a busy and prosperous place with many shops and hotels; apart from the Téléphérique des Glaciers de la Meije it has few ostentatiously modern buildings, and it is one of the most attractive villages in the Oisans.

Access is from La Grave, on the N91 from Le Bourg-d'Oisans.

The Walk

Take the road leading NE from the village street signposted to the *Eglise Romaine* and the chapel; a notice indicates a variety of walks in the area, including Ventelon 1,773m (5,817ft) 40 minutes; Les Hières 1,788m (5,866ft) 1 hour; Valfroide 1,870m (6,135ft) 1 hour 30 minutes; Les Terrasses 45 minutes; Signal de La Grave 2,449m (8,034ft) 3 hours 10 minutes. Continue past the Hôtel des Alpinistes towards the *Eglise Romaine* and the chapel. New buildings here have merged well among the old. Note the stone IHS monogram marked 1634 on the side of the craft workshop, Les Abysses, on the left-hand side of the road: the workshop is open daily and has paintings on wood, candles, pottery and prints of Alpine flowers. Near the church is a fountain; the church itself is twelfth century in origin and has a shallow apse with three tiny lancets; a stone vault and *trompe l'oeil* painting on the plasterwork to make it look like stone; and a beautiful seventeenth century pulpit. The graveyard is full of elaborate memorials. To the side of the church is a little chapel with an elegant tower dated 1746.

Leave the churchyard by the higher gate to the east, and note the house of Dr M Lucher, which has beautiful painted shutters. Turn left, and continue

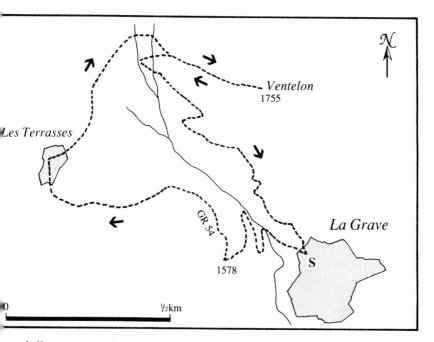

uphill, passing on the left-hand a workshop and craft gallery: its doorway is marked by a *fleur de lys* and the letters IB 1625; and within is an exhibition of Alpine flowers. At the top of the street is a little chapel with a Gothic door and a cross on the roof; over the door is the inscription 'Aide de Piété 1739 '; and, to the left, a hole in the wall set within a heart surmounted by a cross for donations. Beside the chapel is a large cross.

Take the path heading NE uphill from the chapel; a GR sign is painted on the chapel wall just behind the large cross. The track, wide enough at this stage for wheeled vehicles, curves round the hill and crosses the Torrent des Clots. Keep to the hairpins, ignoring the steep path uphill at the first hairpin opposite the church. The terraces are very clear from this point, particularly in the evening light.

Beyond the second hairpin the track becomes a green road and leads round the contour; it is comfortable walking and there are fine views across the valley of the Romanche to the Pic de la Meije and NW to Les Terrasses, its church tower silhouetted against the skyline. The path – GR 54 – climbs the hill north at a steep gradient across the terraces. From here you can hear the clocks of three churches chiming not quite in time. The path approaches the gully of the Torrent des Clots, then turns left towards Les Terrasses. It fords the stream and climbs steadily uphill west to the bottom of the village.

Ventelon from Les Terrasses

The streets in the lower part of the village are unmade, and chickens peck at the ground. A pile of *blettes de fumier* – dried sheep dung to be burnt in the winter – rests against the first house on the left; and brushwood is piled on a wooden balcony. The church is a substantial Romanesque building, looking far too large for the settlement; opposite is a large fountain dated 1901.

From the church turn right, passing the Auberge Ensoleillée (menus at FF60; *raclette* FF65; *fondue* FF55). Follow the minor road from Les Terrasses to Ventelon; at the junction with the road from La Grave bear left to the village, passing below a Swiss-style chalet, the Hôtel La Chaumine. The houses in Ventelon are mainly modern, and the village is by no means as picturesque as Les Terrasses. There are however some older houses, and on the right of the village street beyond the bar restaurant is a curious wall of woven straw. The village has a tiny chapel with a corrugated iron roof and a bellcote on a knoll. There are three collecting boxes in the wall, one for souls in purgatory; one for the upkeep of the building; and one for the *tronc* (fund) *de St Antoine de Padoue*.

Return along the lower road to the left, past an old house with verandahs and *blettes de fumier* and a well built into the hillside, to reach the road beneath the hotel. Walk west towards Les Terrasses until you reach the end of the crennelated wall above the Torrent des Clots. Here, take the track heading downhill towards the terraces. At the second hedge a path leads downhill SE. Take this down past the terraces, which were originally laid out for wheat, but are now used for vegetables or, more often, for hay. The path heads steeply down towards the top end of the village of La Grave, past a concrete reservoir marked 1954, to reach the Gothic chapel some two hours after the start of your walk.

Walk 28   La Grave to Vallons de la Meije

Map no	IGN 3435 est
Distance	6.25km (3.8 miles)
Ascent	600m (1,968ft)
Walking time	4 hours
Grading	Moderate (4)

This walk offers a steep climb towards the base of the Glacier de la Meije. It is hard going but very rewarding, and there are superb views, both to the glacier, and across the valley of the Romanche to the hamlets of Les Terrasses, Ventelon and Les Hières and the mountains to the north of La Grave.

Access is from La Grave, on the N91 from Le Bourg-d'Oisans.

The Walk

As you walk east through the village from the *téléphérique* take a little road downhill to the right just past the Cornet d'Amour – an ice-cream parlour in a fifteenth century chapel. Pass in front of the Restaurant Au Vieux Guide – well worth a visit – then turn right and walk steeply downhill towards a campsite. The road leads back to the right, past a smallholding, to reach a small bridge across the River Romanche. This marks the boundary of the Parc National des Écrins. Turn right to cross a stream rushing fast over rapids – the Torrent du Tabuchet – and take the path to your left leading up the left bank of the stream. The path leads ESE up a moderate gradient, then turns sharp right away from the torrent. The church clock of La Grave struck noon twice as we left the torrent.

After the bend the path becomes quite steep. A tricolour is painted on a rock above the path to indicate that you are within the national park; and the first station on the *téléphérique* is visible ahead of you on the shoulder of the mountain. The rock here is an unattractive grey schist; and the dust on the path is grey. As you walk SW the peak of La Meije appears high above you half left. The path is crossed by another path from the village; a signpost marks the Refuge Chancel ahead, and the Val Chal Vachère to the left. From

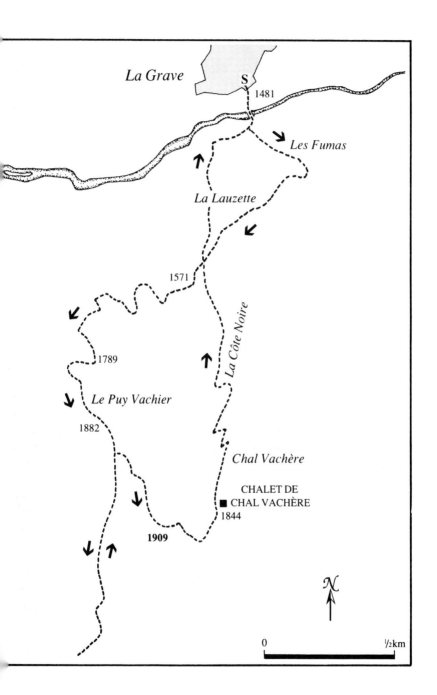

La Grave

S
1481

Les Fumas

La Lauzette

1571

La Côte Noire

1789

Le Puy Vachier

1882

Chal Vachère

CHALET DE
■ CHAL VACHÈRE
1844

1909

N

0 ½km

La Meije

the crossing of the paths are fine views of the gorges of the Maurian Torrent leading into the hills north of La Grave.

Continue on the path towards the Refuge Chancel to the bridge over the Torrent de La Béous – a massive, ugly bridge made of corrugated iron and wood. You may, however, think kindly of it when you cross the same torrent on a bridge of treetrunks higher upstream. Beyond the bridge the path leads up the left bank of the torrent, then hairpins away from it to pass through a gateway made out of a brass bedstead. Continue ahead uphill; then curve round to the left by a little meadow and follow the path uphill, marked by faded waymarks, to reach a combe. A path leads ahead across the combe to the intermediate station of the *téléphérique*; another turns left to follow the south side of the combe. Follow either path – the former is steeper and the latter longer and passes rowan trees and a red square mark on the rocks. Where they join, the path heads briefly WNW, then turns south on a hill opposite the intermediate station. From here is climbs steeply uphill across grassland at 1,789m (5,869ft); there are pleasant level places suitable for a picnic, and fine views across to the Plateau d'Emparis (Walk 26). The climb takes about an hour; and the *alpage* is 372m (1,220ft) from the valley floor.

Cross the *alpage*, climbing steadily uphill, and turn right into the woods to climb towards the cables of the *téléphérique*. Just beyond a red triangular waymark on a rock the path divides, and the path to the right leads towards the Refuge Chancel. Take the path leading uphill SE, with a meadow to its right and the glacier visible ahead. From this point the edge of the glacier looks blue; and its *séracs* (ice peaks) can be clearly seen on the skyline to the left of the sharply pointed Arête de la Meijette.

A signpost at 1,882m (6,174ft) marks another path to the Refuge Chancel to the right and the Vallons de la Meije to the left. Take the path to the Vallons de la Meije, passing a ruined chalet; there is a blue triangle waymark on a dry stone wall to the right as you pass the ruins. Climb steeply to reach a shoulder some 100m further on; from here there is a spectacular view of the glacier. A path leads off to the left at this point; but continue uphill due south towards the glacier.

The path reaches a flattish meadow sheltered by trees, and continues slightly downhill through a pinewood to reach a fork after a short descent. Take the upper fork, marked by white and blue diamonds on a tree to the right of the path. It climbs quite steeply, approaching a scree slope on the right and curving round the southern end of the scree. From here it climbs steeply up rocks from which there are fine views to the glaciers. The whole place is loud with the sound of falling meltwater; and there is a coolness in the air even on the warmest days.

Retrace your steps for about 15 minutes to the point just below the ruined chalet, taking care to take the upper fork just past the tree with the white and blue diamonds. From here a path leads SE around the side of the hill and through woods to cross the Torrent de La Béous; it is newly made, following the line of an older path just downhill, and is marked with blue waymarks on the trees. There are marmots in the woods: listen for their shrill cry, and keep your eyes open for them; they have a reddish-brown pelt, their underside somewhat lighter, and are very well camouflaged.

The path swings right to approach the torrent. Head upstream until you reach a bridge made of four treetrunks rolled together; it is safer than it looks. On the other bank of the torrent is a well-made path leading upstream towards the glacier, and downstream towards the Chalet de Chal Vachère. The path fords a number of ice-cold streamlets coming down the mountainside from the glacier. To the left the torrent falls into a gorge.

The chalet was closed in 1989 but is due to reopen in 1990. From it take the path which is closer to the stream; it leads downhill between a shoulder of hill on the right and a bank on the left; far below and ahead of you is the village. The path descends in broad hairpins, drawing level with a chalet on the other side of the torrent and passing a park bench perched improbably on a knoll. It reaches some trees and joins the point on the ascent where the paths crossed above the bridge over the Torrent de La Béous. Continue ahead, steeply downhill on a narrow path across the meadow of La Lauzette. At the bottom of the meadow it swings right to join the road along the left bank of the Romanche; follow the road upstream to the bridge across the river where you entered the national park, and retrace your steps to La Grave.

Walk 29   Les Cours and Lac du Pontet

Map no	IGN 3435 est
Distance	5km (3 miles)
Ascent	203m (666ft)
Walking time	$1^1/_2$ hours
Grading	Easy (1)

This is an easy walk to a pleasant lake beneath the Clot des Châtellerets. There are fine views down the valley of the Romanche to La Grave and beyond, and southwards to the mountains at the Source of the Romanche (Walk 30), and the hamlet of Les Cours is virtually unspoilt.

Travel via the D91 from Villar d'Arène and thence the D3071 to Les Cours.

The Walk

The walk starts at the village fountain of Les Cours. Walk west along the street and follow the minor road signposted to the Lac du Pontet. A footpath to the left of the road leads to the Chapelle de St Antoine, standing attractively on a knoll – well worth a diversion – a small, empty chapel, its last curé died in an avalanche, and it is hardly used nowadays.

The road to the Lac du Pontet is narrow and unlikely to be busy. The gradient uphill is steep; the road hairpins above the village of Les Cours, giving a bird's-eye view of the roofs. The road passes a brown chalet on the right and reaches a car park. (Those with small children may wish to bring their cars this far, although that does restrict your return journey.)

At the further end of the car park the track divides; the fork to the right is signposted to Lac du Pontet; that to the left to L'Aiguillon and Valfroide. Take the right-hand track, which hairpins uphill towards the hamlet of Le Chazelet 1,897m (6,224ft) – no more, in fact, than a scatter of chalets. To the north, above the lake, is the Clot des Chamois 2,674m (8,773ft) and, higher still, the Pic des Trois Evêchés 3,116m (10,223ft).

The track leads across open hillside towards a large rock. Take the little path leading uphill by a dry water course to reach a bank; the lake is beyond

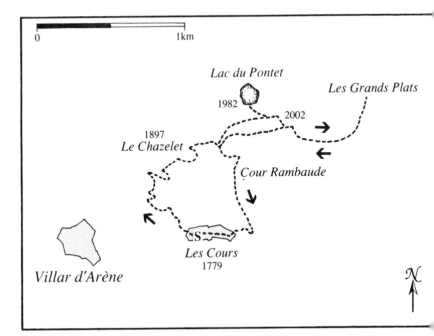

this to the left. It is a favourite spot for trout fishing and for picnics; and in summer is an attractive bathing place. Its eastern end is shallow and choked with reeds – a haunt of dragon-flies which shimmer in the sunlight.

Take the path from the SE corner of the lake, across a small stone dam, and SE through the grassland. The path climbs the shoulder of a hill, then levels off before climbing another shoulder at Les Grands Plats. From here there are wide views up to the source of the Romanche (Walk 30) and to the glaciers above it; the waterfall at the start of the walk where the river falls from the Plan de l'Alpe is clearly visible. Below the waterfall is the settlement of Le Pied du Col, and, below Le Chazelet, the terraces through which you will walk on your return to Les Cours.

Return from the shoulder to the first right-hand bend in the path, at the point where it swings from north to west. Here there is an old path leading towards Le Chazelet, just visible in the grass. (We were told that many of the paths in the area were falling into disuse because the farmers no longer used them to take their cattle to the grazings.) Follow this SW across the hillside; at some points it is stony, and was once well made. It curves round to join a green road which winds downhill towards Le Chazelet. Just before you reach the track leading up to the Lac du Pontet, turn left to take a path trending downhill ESE to the Cour Rambaude. The path reaches a grassy track; follow

142

Les Cours

this downhill east towards a small, fenced enclosure on the hillside. As it approaches an electric fence on the right-hand side it bears right to head steeply downhill south. There are many tumbled stones in the track, and the walking is not easy here.

The route leads down towards two pylons, beyond which is the village of Pied du Col; a path is visible leading through the grass just ahead of the pylons. Continue downhill to meet that path, then turn right on the well-made cart-track which leads west down the terraces towards the eastern end of the village of Les Cours.

The chapel of St Antoine

The track leads behind a row of houses and by a Swiss-style chalet, and turns left to emerge by a fountain. Further down the village street is an attractive old house with a balcony and a sundial dated 1961; its motto '*Vita fugit sicut umbra* ' (Life flees like the shadow). There are three dates on the house – 1774, the date when it was built; 1906, when it was rebuilt after a great fire; and 1961 when it was acquired by the present owner, the sundial maker. Beyond is a little chapel dedicated to Sainte Brigitte; a holy water stoup is outside the door and, on the tiny altar, faded flowers. (We learnt from the owner of the 1774 house that the key of the chapel has gone astray and no one can enter to change the flowers.) Regrettably, Électricité de France have constructed an ugly concrete substation hardly by the western wall of the chapel. Beyond, another sundial with the motto '*Souviens toi de vivre* ' (Don't forget to live) and some pleasantly restored houses.

Walk 30   Source de la Romanche

Map no	IGN 3436 est
Distance	17km (10.5 miles)
Ascent	482m (1,581ft)
Walking time	7 hours
Grading	Moderate (4)

A long walk along a river valley to the source of the River Romanche. There are some steep climbs alongside waterfalls; and the walk gives fine views of glaciers and of the high peaks of the Ecrins. Marmots may be seen on the grasslands.

On the D91 take the D2071, 0.25km (300yds) east of Villar d'Arène, signposted to Le Pied du Col; just beyond an oratory after 1km (0.6 miles) fork right on a little road signposted to the campsite at Pont d'Arsine.

The Walk

Take the path from the campsite at Pont d'Arsine waymarked GR54 and signposted towards Col d'Arsine and the Source de la Romanche. There is a little oratory on the left-hand side of the path just beyond the Pont d'Arsine. Continue up the valley on the lower path parallel with the river; the Glacier de la Seille Vieille is visible in the peaks to your right; below, in the valley, are ugly gravel workings partly masked by silver birches and willows.

The path follows along the hillside above the gravel workings; a sign on the left marks the Plantation Louze Mea, in which are numerous tiny fir trees. Ahead, on the right-hand side of the valley, is the Torrent de l'Homme, falling steeply down from the Glacier de l'Homme. Below you is a car park which can be reached by a track along the valley floor to avoid the 15 minute walk from the campsite to this point.

The path leads across an ugly stretch of mud and slate to approach the narrowing of the valley; from here it curves under the gloomy cliff of Les Crevasses, marked by a red and white waymark on a rock to the left. The path becomes steeper as it reaches the Torrent de l'Homme and climbs up steep

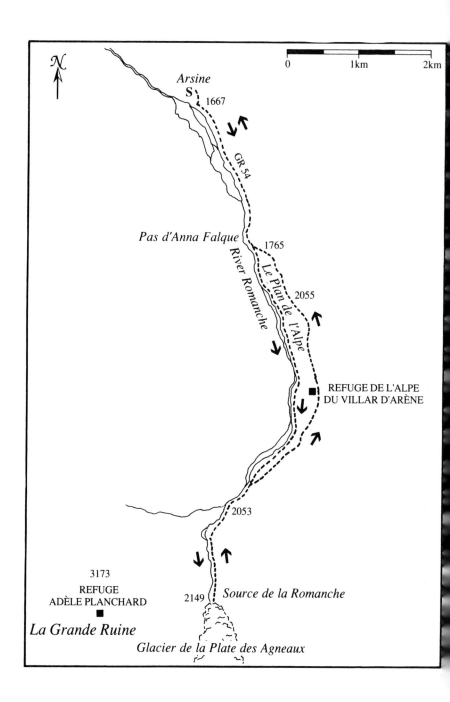

rocks before levelling off slightly above a narrow gorge through which the river tumbles in a fierce cascade.

The path crosses the Ruisseau du Colombier on a plank bridge and heads up in steep hairpins – the fiercest climb of the walk. Ahead is a cascade on the Ruisseau du Colombier – at this point, indeed, you are surrounded by waterfalls. A 5 minute climb takes you to the top of the first series of hairpins, from which there is a spectacular view of the waterfall where the Romanche tumbles into the Pas d'Anna Falque. After a further 5 minutes you reach a signpost pointing left to the Refuge de l'Alpe and Col d'Arsine and right to the Refuge du Pavé and the Refuge Planchard. Take the right-hand path, which is marked with blue waymarks. Cross a little stream on stepping stones, and head uphill immediately opposite; there is a small cliff to the right, and at one point wooden steps built into the hillside. The path crosses tumbled rocks and the walking here becomes quite tough; then it becomes easier through a steep meadow rich in flowers. Towards the top of this *alpage* bear right; a stone arrow points up the hill and the path here is marked by small cairns. After a few metres it swings round to approach the river, at one point heading NW, and then SE to approach the plateau of the Plan de l'Alpe. In all, the climb to the plateau takes some 30 minutes.

A blue and red waymark marks the path as it reaches the Plan de l'Alpe on a section cut through the living rock. The Plan de l'Alpe is a long plateau of flat grassland curving gently to the right between vast mountains, the river spreading through it in wide meanders. Fork right where a cart track meets the path to head towards an electricity substation and the Tête de l'Alpe. To the SE of the valley can be seen the Glacier d'Arsine underneath the Montagne des Agneaux 3,664m (12,021ft); directly ahead, apparently closing the head of the valley above the Tête de l'Alpe, are the Pics de Chamoissière 3,016m and 3,045m (9,895ft and 9,990ft) and the Pic du Dragon 3,229m (10,594ft). The valley of the Romanche heads round to the right beneath the Pic de Chamoissière; to the left the GR54 heads towards the Col d'Arsine and the village of Le Monêtier-les-Bains.

Walk up towards the head of the valley, noting the cascades coming down the surrounding mountains, and cross a tiny bridge, made out of turf on a semi-circle of corrugated iron, to enter a part of the valley littered with rocks and boulders. The path is marked from time to time with blue waymarks; towards the head the valley begins to close in and the path works its way through massive boulders which are, however, dwarfed by the surrounding mountains, the glaciers shimmering on their shoulders, the great scree slopes falling away to the valley floors. Above, on the left, is the Refuge de l'Alpe de Villar d'Arène. Cross a stream on two planks and continue up the valley,

Pas d'Anna Falque

ignoring the path leading uphill left to the Refuge. After the stream the valley becomes less rocky for a few metres; near the head of the valley there is a great pile of rocks.

The river here divides into many channels of very clear water, and the path follows along one of these, past a green lake, and up over stones at a gentle gradient. An ancient rusty signpost marks the point where a path crosses the Romanche to the Refuge du Pavé. The river, narrow here between silver and grey rocks, flows through a natural arch – converted somewhat by man to form a bridge. You continue westwards however up the right bank of the river, which rushes across rapids. A French tricolour painted on a rock to the left indicates that you are in the Parc National des Ecrins. The path levels off to where a new bridge has been built across the river. Over the bridge to the right is the Refuge du Pavé and the Col du Clot des Cavales. Continue on the right-hand bank of the river towards the Source de la Romanche, Refuge Adèle Planchard and Glacier de la Plate des Agneaux.

Continue upstream to a steep valley running southwards with the glacier at its head; the waymarks here are red. A wealth of Alpine flowers flourishes on the meadows leading up to the left of the path, and there are many tiny butterflies and birds. The path leads up the valley through tumbles of boulders and crosses the Romanche – now little more than a stream – on stepping stones to pick its way up through two arms of the river. It crosses over on a plank bridge, and arrives at the foot of a steep rock. Beyond is another meadow leading up to a scree slope at the foot of the glacier. The waters of the river gush from the scree in a multitude of places, so that it is impossible to define a single point at which is its source; but on the left-hand side of the valley is a point where incredibly cold water gushes out with particular force. The climb to the source is of 482m (1,581ft) and takes some 3 hours of steady walking.

It is possible to continue along the bottom of the glacier, turning west and then north to reach the Refuge Adèle Planchard by way of La Grande Ruine. There is a ski route from the refuge to the path to the Source of la Romanche; but walkers should retrace their steps from the source to the Plan des Alpes. From here it is possible to take the same path to the start of the walk, or to take an alternative route by way of the Refuge de l'Alpe de Villar d'Arène, where it is possible to buy food and drink. The refuge and surrounding chalets are clearly visible on the ridge above the Tête de l'Alpe as you walk down the valley; the path to the refuge leads uphill between two upright boulders just beyond the bridge of turf and corrugated iron which you crossed on your ascent.

From the shoulder of the hill is a fine view of the hanging valley of Le Plan de l'Alpe; a cairn at the top, reached after a 10 minute climb from the valley floor, is dedicated to the memory of Spartacus Paysie, 21 July 1929. A signpost near the refuge marks GR54. The refuge, which is the property of the Club Alpin Français, has a range of food and drink, including *vin rouge* at FF22.50 a litre and *omelette nature* FF21. Overnight accommodation is FF56, half-price for members of the Club Alpin.

Two shepherds live here in the summer months; and we saw a couple of tethered donkeys – the tethers were necessary, so we were told, to prevent the donkeys straying down to the campsite, where the food was better and they had taken a liking to tent-pegs. There are a number of ruined buildings here, attesting to more extensive use of the place for summer pastures in former times, as well as two or three restored houses, each with its solar panels facing optimistically southwards.

The path leads NNE along the ridge above the Plan de l'Alpe towards a weather station on a little knoll. It crosses a torrent flowing swiftly down a steep gully by way of a broken wooden bridge, and then forks. Take the upper fork, crossing an earthen track leading down into the Plan de l'Alpe and noting the tricolours painted on the rocks and also on green wooden posts. The path passes beneath the weather station – the *Station Météo du Plan de l'Alpe* – and crosses over fine cropped turf to reach a signpost pointing down to Villar d'Arène, back to Refuge de l'Alpe, Col d'Arsine and GR54, and, across the hill to the right, to Col du Lautaret, from which an alternative, and somewhat easier path, leads to the Plan de l'Alpe and the Source de la Romanche. Take the path towards Villar d'Arène; the campsite where the walk began becomes visible to the NW as you descend steeply past a cairn, and then very steeply on hairpins to rejoin the track on which you made your ascent at the Ruisseau du Colombier.

APPENDICES

I Further Information

Post and Telephone Services

Stamps are for sale in many *tabacs* and paper shops, as well as in post offices. A stamp of FF2.10 will send a letter anywhere in the European Community. It is advisable to send postcards in envelopes to speed their delivery.

Public telephones use coins – minimum FF1 – and phone cards (*Télécartes*) – available for sale in many *tabacs*. Card phones have an electronic sign which asks you to wait while your card is checked, then instructs you to dial; – *Numérotez SVP*. It is possible to telephone from most bars and restaurants. There is a range of tariffs: full tariff from Monday to Friday 8am–12.30pm and 1.30pm–6pm, and Saturday 8am–12.30pm; a 30 per cent reduction Monday to Friday 12.30pm–1.30pm and 6pm–9.30pm, and Saturday 12.30pm–1.30pm; a 50 per cent reduction Monday to Friday 6am–8am and 9.30pm–10.30pm, Saturday 6am–8am and 1.30pm–10.30pm, and Sunday 6am–10.30pm; and a 65 per cent reduction every night from 10.30pm–6am.

The ringing tone consists of a series of long 'beeps'; the engaged tone of rapid short 'bip bip bip bips'.

International dialling codes from France are:

UK	19 44
US	19 1
Canada	19 1
Australia	19 61
New Zealand	19 64
Japan	19 81

After dialling 19 wait for the international dialling tone before dialling the remainder of the number – otherwise you will get the engaged tone. Do not dial the initial '0' of the Area Code of the country you are telephoning. (For example, a call to Glasgow – STD code 041 – would be dialled 19 44 41 111 1111.)

Other useful numbers are:
Operator   10
International Operator   19 33 11
Directory Enquiries   12

Emergency Services

Dial 17 for police, fire, ambulance or mountain rescue (*Secours en Montagne*).
The police can advise both on pharmacies which are open outside normal shopping hours, on the addresses of doctors and can render first aid.
The following are the telephone numbers of police stations in the area:

Chamrousse   76 77 24 46
Grenoble   76 40 44 40
Monestier-de-Clermont   76 34 01 21
Quaix   76 75 30 93
St-Pierre-de-Chartreuse   76 88 60 02
Villard-de-Lans   76 95 11 23

Weather

Weather forecasts for the region may be had by telephoning 76 51 11 11.
Many Syndicats d'Initiative post the daily weather forecast in their windows.

Holidays and Festivals

France has the following national holidays:

1 January
Easter Monday
1 May
8 May
Ascension Day
Whit Monday
14 July
15 August
Weekend of 1 November
11 November
25 December

If a festival falls either on a Thursday or a Tuesday, the French will usually 'bridge' the weekend (*faire le pont*) taking in as holiday the day leading to or following the Sunday.

Consulates in France

The nearest British Consulate is in Lyons: HM Consulate General, 24 rue Childebert, 69288 Lyon: tel 78 37 59 67; fax: 33 72 40 25 24. Hours: Summer 8am–11.30am; 1pm–4.30pm; Winter 9am–12.30pm; 2pm–5.30pm.

The British Consulate General in Paris is at 16 rue d'Anjou, 75008 Paris: tel 42 66 91 42. Hours: 8.30am–noon; 1pm–4.30pm..

The US Consulate in Lyons is at 7 quai Général Sarrail, Lyon 6: tel 78 24 68 49. Hours 9am–noon; 4.30pm–5pm.

French Consulates

24 Rutland Gate, London SW7: tel 071 581 5292
Visa Section, 29-31 Wright's Lane, London W8: tel 071 937 1202
7-11 Randolph Crescent, Edinburgh: tel 031 225 7954
523-535 Cunard Building, Pierhead, Liverpool: tel 051 236 8685
3 Commonwealth Avenue, Boston, MA 02116: tel 617 266 1680
Visa Section: 20 Park Plaza, Statler Building, 6th Floor, Boston, MA 02116:
    tel 617 451 6755
540 Bush Street, San Francisco, CA 94108: tel 415 397 4330
934 Fifth Avenue, New York, NY 10021: tel 212 606 3688
2 Élysée Close, Bonaventura, Montreal BP202 Quebec H5A 1B1:
    tel 514 878 4381
291 George Street, Sydney, New South Wales 2000: tel 29 47 78 or 29 47 79

French Government Tourist Offices

178 Piccadilly, London W1V 0AL: tel 071 493 6594
610 Fifth Avenue, New York NY10020–2452: tel 212 757 1125
1 Hallidie Plaza, #250 San Francisco CA94102: tel 415 986 4161
645 North Michigan Avenue, #630 Chicago IL60611: tel 312 337 6301
1981 Av McGill College, #490 Montreal, Quebec H3A 2W9:
    tel 514 288 4264
1 Dundas Street West, #2405 Box 8, Toronto, Ontario M5G 1Z3:
    tel 416 593 4717

c/o UTA Kindersley House, 33 Bligh Street, Sydney NSW 2000:
   tel 612 231 5244

Tipping

The vast majority of hotels, restaurants and bars add a service charge of 15 per cent to the bill, which will be marked *Service Compris*. No further tips are required, although many people leave the small change.

   A tip of 10 per cent to 15 per cent is appropriate for taxi drivers, although it is not so common to tip taxi drivers in France as in Britain.

II Public Transport

The following lists the walks which are accessible by public transport and their nearest public transport facilities.

Walk

1 La Bastille Walk starts near centre of Grenoble, approached by town bus services or tram.

2 Le Rachais *Téléphérique* to la Bastille.

3 Tour Sans Venin From Tour Sans Venin; Bus Service 510 Grenoble Gare Routière to Villard de Lans and Corrençon via St-Nizier; journey time approximately 35 minutes.

4 Bois de Claret From Méaudre; Service 510 to Lans-en-Vercors (as above Walk 3); change for service to Méaudre.

5 Bellecombe From Autrans; Service 510 to Lans-en-Vercors as above; change for service to Autrans.

6 Charande From Autrans as above Walk 5, combining Walks 5 and 6.

9 Chauplane From St-Michel-les-Portes; train.

10 La Roche From Monestier-de-Clermont; train.

12 La Pinéa From Sarcenas or Col de Palanquit; Bus Service 714 from Grenoble Gare Routière and Square Dr Martin; journey time approximately 40 minutes.

13 Charmant Som From Col de Porte; Bus Service 714 as above; journey time approximately 55 minutes.

14 Col de la Charmette From Col de Porte as for Walk 13; it will be necessary to rearrange the walk to start and finish here.

15 Grande Chartreuse From La Correrie; Bus Service Cars de Chartreuse (tel: 76 50 81 18) from Grenoble Gare Routière to St-Pierre via St-Laurent-du-Pont; journey time approximately 1 hour.

16 Grand Som As for Walk 15.

17 Les Adrets From Les Adrets; Bus Service Brun Autocars (tel: 76 09 64 27) from Grenoble Gare Routière to Prapoutel; journey time 1 hour.

21	Lac Achard	From Chamrousse Roche Béranger; Bus Service 601; Grenoble Gare Routière to Chamrousse; journey time 1 hour 15 minutes.
22	Cascade de l'Oursière	From les Seiglières; Bus Service 601 as for Walk 21; journey time 50 minutes.
23	River Sarenne	Start and finish walk at Huez; Bus Service 302 from Grenoble Gare Routière to Bourg d'Oisans, Huez and Alpe d'Huez; journey time 1 hour 15 minutes.
24	Lac Blanc	As for Walk 23 to Alpe d'Huez; journey time 1 hour 45 minutes; then *télécabine* to Lac Blanc; or as for Walk 23 to Huez; *télécabine* to Alpe d'Huez; *télécabine* to Lac Blanc.
25	Barrage du Chambon	From Chambon; Bus Service 306 from Grenoble Gare Routière to Briançon; journey time 1 hour 25 minutes.
26	Plateau d'Emparis	It is possible to approach the Plateau d'Emparis from La Grave (*see* below Walk 27) by way of GR54. This would require an overnight stay in the Plateau.
27	La Grave	From La Grave; Bus Service 306 Grenoble Gare Routière to Briançon; journey time 1 hour 45 minutes.
28	Vallons de la Meije	From La Grave as above Walk 27.
29	Lac du Pontet	From Villar d'Arêne; Bus Service 306 Grenoble Gare Routière to Briançon; journey time 1 hour 50 minutes.
30	Source of the Romanche	From Villar d'Arêne, as for Walk 29.

III   Gratin Dauphinois

Professor Pierre Laszlo
(*Professeur de Chimie à l'Ecole Polytechnique*)

(Serves four; $1^1/_2$ hours preparation; 3 hours cooking)

Take an earthenware bowl. Crush a clove of garlic against the bottom and sides. Then, using shavings of butter (about 1 oz), grease carefully the whole inner surface of the container. Start slicing 3lbs of potatoes (they ought to be of a fine-grained and compact variety). *The slices must be paper thin* to the extent of being translucent.

Spread the slices in a layer. Season with salt and a liberal amount of freshly-ground pepper. Separate each layer with a spread of heavy cream. When you are through, seal the *gratin* with a final layer of grated Swiss cheese.

Put in the oven, with the temperature initially very hot (450°F). After 20 minutes or so, lower the temperature to 275°F and continue the cooking for another $2^1/_2$ hours. The *gratin* will be ready when a knife blade emerges dry.

Gratin Dauphinois can be served either as the main dish, or as an accompaniment to a meat dish. Any full-bodied red wine (Côtes du Rhône, Burgundy, Cahors, Cabernet Sauvignon, etc) will boost the flavour of this princely dish.

IV Glossary of Topographical Terms

Abri	Shelter
Adret	South facing slope of hillside
Aupet	Little meadow or pasture
Balme, Baume	Cave, Shelter
Barrage	Dam
Bois	Wood
Champs	Field
Chargeoir	Loading bay (eg in a quarry)
Chât, Château	Castle
Chaume	Poor pasture
Clots	Enclosures, cultivated land
Col	Saddle (of a mountain pass)
Colonie de Vacances	Children's holiday camp
Combe	Valley
Crêt	Summit
Croix	Cross
Draye	Natural corridor in a forest, often in the direct line of the slope, down which wood is dragged to the road
Essartage	Clearing made by dragging out or burning the trees
Font, fontaine	Spring
Gouffre	Chasm, gulf
Grange	Barn
Habert	Hamlet on hillside above another village or hamlet
Hameau	Hamlet
Lac	Lake
Lans	Flat area of land
Lauze	Flat rock
Mas	Cottage
Monte-charge	Elevator (eg in quarry workings)
Moulin	Mill
Oeil, Oeille	Small spring
Oratoire	Oratory (usually a small pillar or cross in which there is a niche for a cross or the statuette of a saint or the Virgin)

Pas	Pass, col, saddle
Play, Playe	Maple tree
Pot	A more or less circular depression in the ground, often found in limestone
Ranc, rang	Cliff
Rif	Little stream
Ruisseau	Little stream, burn
Scialet	Crevasse
Serre	Conical bump
Som	Summit
Source	Spring
Source captée	Culverted spring
Télécabine	Cablecar
Télésiège	Chairlift
Téléski	Ski-lift
Usine Hydro Electrique	Hydro-electricity works
Vallon	Valley

V Tourist Offices

Walk

1 & 2 Maison du Tourisme de Grenoble, 14 rue de la Republique: tel 76 54 34 36.

3 As for Walk 1 and Syndicat d'Initiative de St-Nizier, 38250 St-Nizier-de-Moucherotte: tel 76 53 40 60.

4 Syndicat d'Initiative de Méaudre: tel 76 95 20 68.

5 & 6 Syndicat d'Initiative Lans-en-Vercours, 38250 Villard-de-Lans: tel 76 95 42 62.

7 & 8 Syndicat d'Initiative de Rencurel, 38680 Pont en Royans: tel 76 38 97 48 (in winter: tel 76 38 97 32).

9 Syndicat d'Initiative de Gresse-en-Vercours: tel 76 34 01 21; Syndicat d'Initiative de Monestier-de-Clermont: tel 76 34 01 21.

10 As for the second address, Walk 9.

11 As for Walk 1.

12 – 14 Syndicat d'Initiative du Sappey-en-Chartreuse: tel 76 88 84 05; Syndicat d'Initiative de Grenoble: tel 76 54 34 36.

15 & 16 Syndicat d'Initiative de St-Pierre-de-Chartreuse: tel 76 88 62 08.

17 Syndicat d'Initiative de Les Adrets, 38190 Brignoud: tel 76 71 09 94.

18 Syndicat d'Initiative de Prapoutel les Sept Laux, 38190 Brignoud: tel 76 08 17 86.

19 & 20 Syndicat d'Initiative de Theys-en-Belledonne, 38570 Theys: tel 76 71 05 92.

21 & 22 Syndicat d'Initiative de Chamrousse, 38410 Uriage: tel 76 89 92 65.

23 & 24 Syndicat d'Initiative de l'Alpe d'Huez, 38750 l'Alpe d'Huez (Place Paganon): tel 76 80 35 41.

25 Syndicat d'Initiative les Deux Alpes: tel 76 79 22 00.

26 & 27 Syndicat d'Initiative de la Meije, La Grave, Villar d'Arène, 05320 La Grave: tel 76 79 90 05; Bureau des Guides, 05320 La Grave: tel 76 79 90 21.

28 – 30 As for the first address, Walks 26 & 27.